BreakPoints

BreakPoints

Where Businesses Get Stuck
... And How They Get Unstuck!

LARRY KESSLIN & CHRIS WINTER
with Susan Caba

BreakPoints: Where Businesses Get Stuck … And How They Get Unstuck!
by Larry Kesslin and Chris Winter

4-Profit Press
Copyright © 2011, 2013 by 4-Profit LLC

Published by 4-Profit Press, South Salem, NY

To order books in bulk:
BreakPoints@4-Profit.com
4-Profit
PO Box 206
South Salem, New York 10590
www.4-Profit.com

First Edition 2011, Second Edition 2013

ISBN: 978-0-9886592-0-9 (paper)
ISBN: 978-0-9886592-1-6 (ebook)
Library of Congress Control Number: 2011922778

Printed in the United States of America

1) Business   2) Leadership   3) Management   4) Change

We would like to dedicate this book to our families.
Our wives, Ilise and Katie, and our kids, Drew, Noah, Sean and Maggie.
Without their love and support none of this really matters.

Contents

FOREWORD

Ken Blanchard

I've read lots of books about right and wrong ways to run a business. Every so often a book on this topic comes along that really piques my interest. *BreakPoints* is one of those books.

It's a given that as the owner of a newly developing business, you will have growing pains. But when those pains turn into actual obstacles in your path to success, you may need help working around them. Larry Kesslin and Chris Winter have broken through what they see as the seven most critical barriers faced by new business owners. Each of these barriers stands ready to crack—block—young and growing organizations—*BreakPoints* reveals how to avoid them and thrive.

BreakPoints is an interesting and engaging story within a story. Tom Wilcox is a successful entrepreneur who has been asked to be a guest lecturer for a graduate-level business class. He tells the students the story of how he and his business partner overcame seven distinct obstacles—what they refer to as *breakpoints*—on the way to becoming successful business owners.

These seven *BreakPoints* would have been good to know about when my wife, Margie, and I cofounded The Ken Blanchard Companies® with a small group of talented colleagues more than thirty years ago. Fortunately, our organization survived these seven critical junctures, but Larry and Chris' insights would have made things easier.

Thanks to *BreakPoints*, you don't have to do it the hard way. By learning from others' experiences—both good and bad—you can keep your organization growing and going on the right path toward long-term success. Larry and Chris have the experience and knowledge to help you succeed. Let them share their wisdom with you—you'll be glad you did.

> Ken Blanchard
> Coauthor of *The One Minute Manager*®
> and *Leading at a Higher Level*

INTRODUCTION

Welcome to Leadership 301

"I'm going to tell you about the seven ways we almost screwed up our business before we ever got it going—the seven Break-Points that, had we not been able to recover, I most likely wouldn't be here today talking to you about success."

Tom Wilcox rolled up the left sleeve of his shirt, exposing his arm up to his elbow.

"See that?" he said, pointing to the skin on the outside of his arm. A dozen or so graduate students looked at his arm, then back at his face. Their fingers were poised over laptop keyboards, waiting to record imparted wisdom.

"Oh, you don't see it!" he said, rolling down the sleeve and pacing at the front of the room.

"What about this?" he asked abruptly, turning his head so the class could view the side of his neck. "See that?" he said, gesturing toward his carotid artery.

"No? *Still* don't see it?" Tom pulled his shirt tail from the back of his pants and reached for his belt buckle.

Tom stopped. He grinned.

"What I'm showing you—and what you're not seeing— are my scars. My entrepreneurial scar tissue," he said. "Oh, that's right! It's invisible! I forgot—you can't see it until I *tell* you about it. But believe me, it's there.

"Because starting a business, especially your first business, is a rough experience. No matter how good you are, you're going to get banged up a little, maybe break a few bones, collect some cuts and bruises. It's like any sport. The harder you go at it, the better you want to be at it, the more likely you are to take some necessary risks—and sustain some injuries.

"And that's where the entrepreneurial scar tissue comes in. I'm going to show you—don't worry! As I said, it's invisible!— my scar tissue. If you see mine, learn how I got it; the idea is you won't have to get yours the same way."

Tom—a tall man in an open-necked striped business shirt and khakis, with neatly styled hair neither blond nor gray, and wire rimmed glasses neither offensively dated nor ostentatiously stylish—appeared nondescript in every way. Which only made his comments about "invisible scar tissue" seem even more bizarre.

"Notice that I'm not saying you won't get *any* scar tissue. I'm just saying you might be able to avoid the potholes and pitfalls that gave me mine.

"I know, you're hoping to hear something like the Seven Steps on the Pathway to Success, aren't you?" he said, approaching first one then another of the students in the front row. "But I'm not going to talk so much about the steps to success.

"I'm going to tell you about the seven ways we almost screwed up our business before we ever got it going—what I call the seven BreakPoints on an entrepreneur's journey; the places that businesses get stuck in the mud, stalled, bogged down. Oddly enough, the places where they get stuck, rarely do businesses even realize they're stuck ... or why. Those are the places where entrepreneurs and their businesses begin to die slowly, without even recognizing they are dying.

"If you can recognize these *BreakPoints*—if you have the foresight to spot them and avoid even approaching them—you will have vastly increased your chances of success.

"Now, I can lay out those seven points of peril for you—and I will.

"But it's been my experience that we all read lists or maps and we don't 'get' them. Instead, I'm going to tell you my story. It's a success story, sure—in the end."

Tom patted his chest as though patting a pocketed check. At 50-something, he and his partner, Jose Alvarez, had recently sold MicroVision Technology Group, which they'd built from scratch, for a cool bundle of cash—eight figures, right to the bank. For the moment, they were just "chilling." Tom dreamed of playing all the best golf courses in the world; Jose's goal was to attend baseball games in every major league stadium in one season.

In the meantime, Tom agreed to teach an eight-week seminar in the Graduate School of Business. To the eager, would-be business owners in the class, he personified what they hoped would be their own highly successful futures.

"Yeah, you're all gonna be just as successful as we were—I hope," Tom continued, as though reading their minds.

"But to help get you there, I'm going to focus on those potential breaking points; the times and places that we came close to losing everything we were working for. Why? Because I really believe we learned the best lessons when we came close to failing. I hope that, by learning from my mistakes, you'll be able to enhance and speed your own successes.

"So. There won't be a textbook for this class. Instead, we'll read a true confession of sorts that I've written about my entrepreneurial journey. Each week, we'll explore an obstacle—or four—I faced along the way."

He tucked his shirt-tail in. "And don't worry, I won't be—well, I probably won't be—asking you to look closely at any physical scars.

"Okay, I don't have a big syllabus to hand out, but I am going to go over the basics with you here a little bit ... give you a preview of the topics we'll be thinking and talking about."

He took out a marker and turned to a "flip chart" on the podium, a large pad of inexpensive paper mounted on an easel—one often used in lectures in place of a white or blackboard.

"Yeah, I know," he said. "Here I am, big IT guy and where's my Power Point deck, right? Sometimes it's just better to go simply and with the basics."

What I'm going to present, I call BreakPoints. If you can recognize them; if you have the foresight to spot them ... and avoid even approaching them—you will have vastly increased your chances of success.

Tom scrawled,

BreakPoint #1
Have a plan, chart your course.

"What do I mean by this? I do mean have a business plan, a fiscal vision and all that good business stuff. What we're going to be going over, though, is broader than that.

"I'm going to be asking you to have a life plan and come up with a vision of what success looks like—to you. What do you want your life to look like when you get to be my age. On top of that, we're going to talk about what your business is going to have to look like for you to achieve that success.

"My philosophy is that your business should be a tool to make your life successful, not vice versa. But that doesn't mean you are going to neglect your business. Nope. You're going to hone your skills so that your business gives you options in life. In order to do that, you have to know what your goal is and what it's going to take to make it happen.

"This is where, in your other classes, you learn metrics and succession planning and all of that. We're not going in depth into those things. But they are important, and we're going to tell you why.

"So, *BreakPoint #1* is failure to make a plan."

He continued to write.

BreakPoint #2
Hire great people,
build your pit crew.

"A lot of people—me, for example—get into business because we're good at something. In my case, I was good at coming up with and providing service solutions to IT companies. Then I decided I could go into business for myself and make a lot more money doing what I was already doing.

"Unfortunately, that's what business guru Michael Gerber describes as 'an entrepreneurial seizure.' In other words, I didn't succeed in making the transition from just providing a service to a much larger job, running a business. I didn't realize it wasn't my job anymore to come up with and provide those services—it was my job to find the best people I could to provide the services, and then manage the business in such a way that they could do their jobs.

"*BreakPoint #2,* then, is failure to realize you've got to give up what you're good at, and let other people do it."

Tom then flipped the page of the flip chart over and wrote:

BreakPoint #3
Know yourself, your leaders, your company, your community.

"This is key, key, key. Let me say it again, this is one of—if not the *most*—important issues you are going to have to deal with as an entrepreneur-business owner. I wish I could sum it up with some terse phrase, but I can't at the moment. Let's call it communication. Any of you Paul Newman fans out there might recognize the phrase, 'What we have here is failure to communicate.' from the classic movie, *Cool Hand Luke*.

"This is where you develop a close-knit leadership team, based on their ability and their commitment to communicate with one another. Except it's more than that—we could spend the entire semester on this topic. BreakPoint #3 is failure to know who you are, what your leadership style is, how people see you, who your company is and how you convey that to the appropriate audience. I call it the "4 Cs of Communication."

"This is where magic and science come together in this mysterious alchemy that results in spectacular leadership."

Tom paused. "If there is one take-away from *BreakPoint #3*, it's probably the necessity of continually encouraging everyone in your company to keep asking the question, *Is this what you meant?*

"I know, I sound like I've been reading too much Eckert Tolle, but I'm telling you, if you can get this concept, not only will your business be more successful, but your life will be more satisfying.

"*BreakPoint #3* is failure to know who you are as a person and a company, followed by the failure to communicate that clearly to your employees and your community."

He turned again to the flip chart pad.

BreakPoint #4
Partnership Pain.

"Guys—and gals," he said, "Choosing business partners is like deciding who to marry. Make the right choice and life can be blissful. Make the wrong choice and, well, it can be like marriage without sex! And—just like marriage—if you make the choice for the wrong reasons, then you will have no *idea* the problems that can develop!

"Unfortunately, this is an area where people can be totally, completely, absolutely ignorant of what they are doing. I've seen a lot of partnerships, good and bad. The problem a lot of partners get into: they haven't thought about the risks of business. They're just thinking about the profits—it's like getting married and forgetting that you're promising to stick it out 'for better or for worse.' Nobody likes to think about the 'for worse' parts.

"So, *BreakPoint #4* is failure to understand the concepts of equity, risk and ownership. Trust me, this is a problem you *really* need to avoid."

Tom flipped the page on the big notepad again.

"Here's where we're really getting into the mature stages of the business. By now, we thought we had it handled. We've been in business a while, things are looking pretty good. And then you realize, hey, 'We're at the edge of a big leap across the chasm. Either we make it or we're small potatoes—or worse, out of business—for the rest of our lives.' That's what the next two *BreakPoints* are about."

BreakPoint #5
Rev the sales engine, scale the business.

"It's all about the sales process," Tom said, capping the marker. "*BreakPoint #5* is where the company has to scale up in order to meet goals. And that means increasing sales to support that scale-up in a predictable way.

"You can't rely on a motley crew of sales people, everyone going their own way. Now is the time to hire an experienced sales manager—with the emphasis on *manager*—who can motivate and lead your sales force.

"Your sales process—the way you recruit, develop, evaluate and manage your people—is the biggie. We'll be talking a lot about how a sales manager is different from a sales person, no matter how good."

He turned again to the flip chart.

BreakPoint #6
Changing of the Guard.

Tom paused, sat on the edge of his table on the podium and looked out at the class. He let the silence linger for a few moments longer than was comfortable.

"At this point, your loyalty is no longer to the people who helped you build this business. Your loyalty now is *to the business*. It's like the difference between your undergraduate degree and your MBA.

"The company is *really* turning professional, with professional standards—and professional managers. You've got processes in place, you can actually step away from the business and pay some attention to your life—and, you know what, you like that. You can almost imagine the business getting along without you! Not quite, but almost.

"That's not to say you don't take care of the people who came on board early. But, if you're more concerned with the lives of Alice in Accounting or Sam in Customer Services than you are about the operation of the business, you are limiting your options.

"The good news? If you've made it this far, you've already taken care of Alice and Sam. They have either increased their skills and found their niche in the company, or you've helped them move on to something that is their next step along their path."

He scrawled again on the fresh flip chart pad:

BreakPoint #7
CEO Time

He turned and capped the marker.

"Are you the person to lead this company?" he asked.

He let a long silence envelop the room.

"What does this company owe you? What do you owe the company? What do you want from the company? Are you an entrepreneur, a business owner or a CEO? Or, are you a mix—do you have traits of each?

"They are not the same thing, you know—the entrepreneur, the business owner and the CEO," he said.

"This is where we come back to the beginning. What do you want from the business? What do you want from life? Who has the skills to deliver what you want—is it you? Or is it someone you hire? Do you want control? Or do you want freedom?"

Tom sat on the edge of his table.

"You are the owner of the business. Do you also need to be the CEO? Is that the best use of your time? Your skills? Your life?

"So here's where the practical nature of business and the philosophical questions of life intersect. Where do you get the most reward? What the hell is reward, anyway? Do you own a business to feed your ego? To meet your lifestyle needs? What gives you satisfaction? Building a great business and being at the helm? Great. Do it. But are you at the helm of a sailboat when the whole idea of the ocean makes you seasick? Could you hire a captain to run the boat while you head for the mountains?

"That's *BreakPoint #7*—CEO Time. You've reached the point of ultimate choice. If you love running the business, if you have the skills—do it. If you've gotten to this point so you can take a year off and literally sail the world—do it.

"If you're lucky, you have attained that freedom every entrepreneur dreams about. You can start a new business. You can devote your life to adventure. You can stick around and lead your current business to new levels of success.

"What my partner and I have achieved—and believe me, it wasn't easy—is that we've arrived at the point that we have those choices. We have the freedom.

"Hell, we're not Bill Gates—we don't have unlimited choices. But we made it through the *BreakPoints*. We managed to keep the kayak upright through the rough waters and we've got options.

"In my mind, that's what we all want in life. Options. I'm here to help you guide your kayaks, to keep you from getting hit in the head too often, to keep you from breaking your arms, to minimize your entrepreneurial scar tissue. So that, when you get the gray hairs I have, you'll have options."

The MTG Story

*Three months and look at this—MTG is makin'
the big bucks!*

Tom Wilcox splashed Budweiser on his father's bald spot, then chugged half the bottle as the old man retaliated by grabbing his son in a mock chokehold. The St. Louis Rams, in a slew of losing seasons, weren't in the running for even a division championship, much less a Super Bowl trophy. Not that the Wilcox men cared that much. The playoffs, no matter the team, were just an excuse for father and son to hang out together.

For as long as Tom could remember, his father had made time to watch end-of-season games with him—an extravagance for a man who spent long days and late nights running the family-owned restaurant in south St. Louis to pay the bills. Tom had put in his own long hours in the restaurant through high school, helping his father with everything from clearing tables to pinch-hitting at the stove when the cook didn't show. The Rams may have tanked but the play-offs seemed an appropriate time for Tom to share a trophy of his own.

"Hey, Dad," he said, as the Fox sportscasters reviewed highlights. "You still have that $5 bill tacked up by the cash register at the bar?"

Tom knew the tattered bill was still there, signifying his father's first profit, along with other mementos marking financial landmarks along the restaurant's road to modest success. At 30, Tom wasn't so sure the rewards had been worth the missed family dinners, the skipped vacations and the sixteen-hour days his father had invested, but he knew the business was a source of pride for his parents. Besides, he was getting a taste himself of the sweetness that sweat equity could impart to a workweek.

"Yeah, what about it?" His father had cleared the beer from the coffee table—much as he would have cleared his bar—and was pulling on a windbreaker to head home.

"Don't tell me you're gonna need that, too, for this deal you and Jose got going?"

The elder Wilcoxes had lent Tom $10,000 a few months earlier to launch MTG, MicroVision Technology Group. In truth, Tom and his partner Jose were the only members of the group. But, as his mother liked to say, they had "potential for growth."

"Hold on a sec." Tom disappeared into his office. Furnished with two desks, a motley array of file cabinets and an eight-foot folding table purchased for $15 at a garage sale and referred to as the "board room," the office was situated in the larger of the apartment's two bedrooms. MTG could, therefore, claim a prosperous-sounding West County address as its headquarters. Tom emerged with two pieces of paper.

He snapped the first, an elongated business check made out to MTG for several thousand dollars, in front of his father. "Payday, Dad! Payday!" he crowed. "Three months and look at this—MTG is makin' the big bucks! Our first official retainer. And it comes with a contract, a yearlong contract for so-luu-tions ser-vices."

Tom drew out the last words, savoring the sibilant sound of success. ("Hey," he'd told Jose earlier that day, when his partner mocked the phrase, "so I'm a nerd—I'm taking pleasure in the little things, okay?")

Before his father could say anything, Tom dropped the check and displayed the second document. It, too, was a business check. The same crisp blue as a button-down shirt and bearing the MTG monogram in the upper left corner, this one was made out in Tom's spiky handwriting to T. William Wilcox for "one thousand dollars and no/100s."

It was check number 0001; Tom had saved it for the first payment on the loan from his father. "It's payback time, Dad," he said, tucking the check into the chest pocket of his father's short-sleeve shirt. "Early payback time."

"Aw, I told your mother you'd be good for it," his father replied. They didn't say anything more, just shook hands and exchanged shoulder punches, then a hug. Tom knew his father couldn't have been more proud if Tom had been Super Bowl MVP or won the Nobel Peace Prize—truthfully, Tom was just about as proud of himself—but neither one was going to say so. Tom's father didn't say a word about the check, but it was never cashed. It was tacked over the register at the restaurant, just above a faded five-dollar bill.

Tom had been working for five years for a small IT firm in St. Louis. He was the company's top salesperson. His friend, Jose Alvarez, was a senior engineer and a whiz at solving technical problems for customers. The two made a great team. When Tom was ready to strike out independently, he invited Jose to come along as junior partner. If and when they ever made money—and Tom had no doubts they would—he'd have 70 percent equity and Jose would have 30 percent.

The two were a lot alike. A year or two older than Tom and single, Jose also grew up in a working class family. After high school, he attended technical school at night while working with his father during the day at the GM plant in north St. Louis.

Jose's dad was his boyhood hero. What the family lacked in money, Mr. Alvarez made up for in creativity. He liked to remind Jose that "it was the days before you threw away anything that didn't work—you fixed it, whether it was the washing machine, the car or the lawnmower. You got your hands dirty and you fixed it." Jose and the rest of the neighborhood boys spent weekends in his father's basement shop, tinkering with old televisions and fans until Mr. Alvarez trusted them to actually take something apart and repair it.

"My dad was the Einstein of mechanical mysteries—like he was the machine-whisperer," he told Tom the first time they took in a few beers and a Cardinals game.

"He gave us crap if he thought we were watching too much television. 'Get down here and fix something for your mother,' he'd yell. The only time I ever saw him stumped was when we got our first computer—no moving parts! I still don't think he understands that I do with computers what he does with cars."

Tom knew his sales success depended on Jose's technical wizardry. Between the two of them, they promised and delivered. He felt sure the combination would spell success if they went out on their own. The more they talked during the first few months of that year, the more he believed in their vision—money, freedom, flexibility. All good, as far as he and

Jose could tell. No downsides, as long as they kept overhead low. How hard could that be?

Finally, after a bit of quiet consultation with a few clients from the old firm and an effort to make sure their VISA bills were cleared, they gave notice. MicroVision Technology Group officially launched two weeks later on a Monday at about 8:30 a.m., when Jose appeared at the door of Tom's apartment with a bag of bagels and a container of cream cheese.

Elation popped like a small firecracker in Tom's chest when he saw Jose coming through the door that first morning. Who knew, he thought to himself, that starting a business could be so simple?

The maples outside Tom's living room window had progressed through the gold of late summer and on to a blazing fall red. He'd already hit the snooze button, the workout room and the shower by the time Jose let himself into the apartment carrying the Monday morning bag of bagels. Tom greeted his partner with something less than the enthusiasm of that first day. Fifteen months into their venture, business was great and their partnership was great. Everything was great.

Except Tom felt less in control of his life than he had as an employee at his old firm. MTG's "board room" had pushed out of the second bedroom and taken over the apartment.

Neither he nor Jose had taken time off for Hawaiian vacations—or even long weekends, despite their early visions of freedom and flexibility.

Amanda, Tom's fiancé, was more than a little irritated at his inability to commit to firm honeymoon plans because he wasn't sure how long he could be away from MTG.

Business was booming—and promised to get even better. There wasn't a company around that didn't depend on ever-increasingly sophisticated technology systems.

Jose's intuitive ability to make these systems work, combined with Tom's charismatic sales approach, added up to satisfyingly full work schedules for the both of them.

In fact, some days were more than satisfyingly full. More clients, the partners were learning, didn't just mean more money. More clients also meant a higher risk of simultaneous emergencies. They had a roster of freelance technicians they could call when the workload threatened to overwhelm Jose, but the hourly cost of using independent contractors quickly ate into profit. Lately, costs seemed to outweigh income more often than not.

"Seriously, Tom," said Jose on this Monday morning, as the two sat at the folding boardroom table. "We've got to bring someone else in. I'm overloaded. If anything unexpected goes down, something is going to hit the floor and splatter."

Tom frowned, an uncharacteristic expression for him. Much as he loved the freedom of working for himself and being accountable to no one, moments like these left him feeling a little panicked. How the hell was he supposed to know what to do? A couple of times in the beginning, he'd called his father for advice. But now the issues were too big for his father to really be able to help. Punting wasn't really working anymore, either.

Reaching for a second bagel, Tom tried a diversionary tactic.

"Yeah, I know, buddy, I know. But we've got to deal first with some of these invoices. I hate to say it, but making all this money, or at least collecting it, is more of a pain in the butt than I realized. And I've booked in a couple more clients who want monthly deliverables. What's your time like for initial visits?"

Jose had a knack for turning his usually warm and laughter-lit brown eyes into Junior Mints—shiny, flat circles devoid of expression. As part of a deadpan joke delivery, the look could be hysterical. At this moment, Tom could see the gaze was meant to be anything but funny. Procrastination was no longer an option. "So," he asked Jose, "got anybody in mind?"

"What did I tell you—he's great, right?"

Tom considered his partner's question. "Yeah, he could really work out," he said.

The two had just met for the first time with Bob Rogers, operations VP at a small St. Louis corporation. Jose knew him from the pre-MTG days. He'd never worked directly with Bob, but he knew Bob's people thought highly of his technical skills.

"He's made VP. That counts for something," said Jose. "He's got experience; I bet he understands operations as well as we do, plus I think he's been taking graduate business classes the last couple years."

Bob's combination of technical skills, corporate experience and—Jose and Tom acknowledged to one another—his college business degree could really add value to MTG. Neither mentioned, though the thought occurred to both, that Bob's age—about 15 years older than either of them—created a comforting paternal aura.

"The thing is," Tom continued, "he must be making at least $100,000, right? No way we can afford that. What could we offer that would be worth turning his back on that kind of money?"

He turned the key in the door of the co-op office suite MTG now occupied. The shared receptionist, joint boardroom and professional atmosphere contributed to their sense of success. Still, without additional help, both knew a single crisis could mean disaster. Jose's workday was stretching beyond 12 hours on a regular basis.

"I'm thinking he might take the pay-cut if he got equity," said Jose. "I floated the idea—no commitment—and I think he might be looking for some kind of security for the future. You know, he's got three kids, I don't think his wife works and at least one of those kids is going to college in a year or two."

"Okay, set up another meeting. Call the guy in, let's see what he wants in his package and when he can start," Tom said, as Jose walked to his own office.

Tom flipped his light, already shuffling the handful of pink telephone messages the receptionist had handed him a few moments earlier. No doubt his email inbox would be full, too. "Yeah, baby! Bring it! Let's double the client list!"

Two weeks later, Tom, Jose and Bob were gathered around Jose's desk. Tom and Jose had congratulated themselves earlier that morning on their decisiveness in bringing Bob on board so quickly. Obviously, they were getting the hang of business.

Bob was not so much stocky as blocky, thought Tom. His face was square, his body was square—he gave the impression of being one of those Lego people, assembled from brick-shaped pieces that snapped together. There was nothing unpleasant about him. He was just bland. The two younger men were, as usual, casually dressed, Tom in khakis and a long-sleeved business shirt and Jose in his customary jeans, Polo shirt and running shoes. Bob wore gray slacks and a tweed jacket, as well as wingtips.

Neither Tom nor Jose owned a pair of wingtips.

This was the trio's third meeting, after a string of emails. Bob had been insistent. He wouldn't leave the security of his corporate gig, not to mention his generous salary, vested pension, 401K and flexible spending plan, without significant equity in MTG. He'd asked for 30 percent, then backed his figure down to 25. No way that was going to happen, Tom told him.

Privately, he and Jose had agreed one night over beers that—considering the company was worth roughly nothing at that point—they would pony up 15 percent. Jose would kick in 5 percent and Tom 10 percent.

"He'll be the junior-junior partner," Jose quipped, as they settled on the percentages.

"Yeah, that's what we'll call him—Junior-Junior," Tom replied.

Bob had pushed a bit longer for 20 percent, then agreed on the offered 15 percent share. This meeting was the official "signing ceremony," bringing Bob on board.

Tom and Jose had pens in hand when Bob raised a final concern.

"No big deal, guys, but what titles are in play here?"
Jose paused and looked up. Tom did the same.

"Whaddya mean?" asked Jose.

"I mean, what are our titles?" Bob asked.

Tom thought he might be joking. "You mean like 'Master of His Own Domain?' 'King of the South County Universe?' 'Ruler of All He Surveys?' 'He Who Bows to No One?'"

Bob looked at him blankly. Jose did his Junior Mint eyes thing, which Tom recognized as the non-verbal equivalent of "Is he kidding?"

"Well, Bob, what did you have in mind?" Tom asked.

"I think vice president of engineering would be appropriate," he responded.

"Yeah. Hmmm. Well." Words failed Tom. "The thing is," he stammered, "we don't have a president. We, uh, haven't really, uh, thought about how ... or what, uh, to call one another ..."

"Except for Jose or Tom," Jose interjected.

"Yeah ..." Tom added. To their credit, neither even thought of bringing up Junior-Junior.

Bob's expression hadn't changed. "What do you have on your business cards?" he asked.

Tom and Jose simultaneously pulled out their wallets, then their MTG business cards. Each looked at the small cream rectangles as though seeing them for the first time. There were their names in 12-point Arial under the MTG logo. No titles, just phone numbers and addresses. They simply hadn't considered titles.

"Idiots," thought Tom.

"Listen," said Jose. "I don't think we're ready to anoint Presidents, Vice Presidents or Speakers of the House—how about if you go with Senior Engineer, Operations? We can haggle later over the titles if we have to."

To Tom's relief, Bob agreed.

"Yeah, man!" thought Tom. "Problem solved. This business is back on the high-speed line to success."

— *The Classroom* —

... we did not understand or think about the implications of giving another person equity in our company.

"What were we *thinking*?"

"Bob Rogers is a great guy, don't get me wrong," Tom continued. "Hiring him was a good decision. He knew the business; he did the work.

"But—and this is a big 'But'—did we know or think about what equity meant? Did we understand the rights and responsibilities that go along with equity? Did we give a moment's consideration to the value of equity? After all, so far as we knew, the company had no monetary value.

"Of course, now I know better," he said, drawing laughter.

"Well, just in case you have any doubts, the answer to those questions is No; we did not understand or think about the implications of giving another person equity in our company. The only thing on our minds was finding someone who could help handle the work. We never thought of long term consequences.

"Even more unbelievably? We didn't even consider asking Bob to invest his own money in the company," Tom said. "We had no idea that having the power to give equity—or better yet, sell it—was a tool we could have used to achieve some of our goals."

On that note, Tom called for a break. "Everyone be back in 20 minutes," he told the group.

When the class reassembled, the students found their chairs had been re-arranged. In some cases, three chairs were clustered

25

together, in others, there were two and yet others, four. There seemed to be no rationale for the arrangements. As they took their seats, the students noticed each group had been furnished with a deck of cards.

"Here's the deal," Tom told them. "We're going to play games—each group is going to play an individual game, resulting in a winner. Then we are going to compare scores between groups, to determine over-all winners.

"The rules are simple. You will have fifteen minutes to complete your game. Those in your seating group constitute your teammates. When I signal the game is about to begin, you will shuffle and distribute your cards.

"Here is the cardinal rule: You may not discuss or define the game you are playing. Whoever is holding the cards at this moment will deal them, according to whatever rules that person thinks is appropriate. No player may ask the name of the game or the directions for playing it. In 15 seconds, the games will start. Each group will determine, based on the moves of the others in his or her team, how the game is played and will play it to the best advantage of the team.

"Ready, set, GO!"

A confused silence settled over the group before students began dealing cards. Low murmurs arose, as players tried to parse the rules of the games being dealt—Poker? Pitch? Bridge? Kings on the Corner? The phrase "Go Fish" was heard arising from one group, indicating those players, at least, had determined the game at hand.

After 15 minutes, Tom called "Stop!" He went from group to group. "Who won?" he asked. "What were you playing?" With the exception of the Go Fish group, few of the groups had been able to determine what game they were playing, let alone who was winning. Comparing scores group-to-group was even more fruitless—it was clear that no two groups had been playing the same game.

"Here's my point," said Tom, after the laughter had died down and the conversational circle had been re-established. "It's hard to win at a game—it's hard to play a game—if you don't know what it is, if you don't know what the rules are; if you don't have a plan.

But when it comes to business, the 'cheats' aren't cheating. They are shortcuts. They are shortcuts to success. They allow you to proceed directly to 'Go.'

"On the other hand, if you know the game or if someone is coaching you on the game from the beginning, you are going to have an advantage. *You* know what the goal is, you know at least roughly what you have to do to reach that goal."

Tom was walking around now, energized by the point he was about to make. "Jose and I have never really been video gamers—I've always been a golfer and Jose manages a fantasy baseball league. But you guys—you guys have grown up on computer games. I don't care if it was Nintendo, PlayStation, XBox, whatever. We could even talk Candy Land or Go Fish.

"What a lot of them have in common is, there are different levels. You make it through one level, and you get to the portal of the next level, then the next and so on and so forth. You get defeated at some point and you have to go back and start over.

"And every time you start over, you get through those first levels faster than you did the first time, the second time, the third. You advance much farther than you did the first time you played.

"And here's the not-so-secret dirty little secret we all learn," he said. "You can go online and look up 'cheats.' You know, the keys to getting through those levels faster, so you don't have to make all the mistakes an un-informed player makes."

He paused. "Well, when you're playing a game—at least I think—using the 'cheats' makes winning less satisfying. You didn't win based on your own skill and intuition.

"But when it comes to business, the 'cheats' aren't cheating. They are shortcuts. They are shortcuts to success. They allow you to proceed directly to 'Go.'

"And that's why I'm here. I don't want you to be stalled at the third portal, looking for the key to the next level. I don't think you need to learn the hard way, figuring out the game and the next move on your own.

"I am here to be your 'cheat'—your guide."

The MTG Story

As a technician, Bob was great, thought Tom.
As an administrator—well ...

"Renee's got to go."

Jose made the remark as Tom took a bite of the roast beef and gorgonzola sandwich in front of him, and Bob consulted a text message from his wife while swigging ice tea. The three were gathered at their de-facto off-site office, the centrally located sandwich shop where they frequently met for mid-day administrative meetings.

"I've been thinking the same thing," said Tom. "Joe Blackburn called me last week and said she'd totally screwed up their billing and then bit Marcy's head off when Marcy called to ask about it."

"Yeah, Joe told me Marcy's on the verge of quitting if she has to keep dealing with Renee," said Jose. "I told Renee last week, look, this is a big client—I don't care if Marcy gives you hives, take a deep breath and deal with it."

"I don't know," said Bob, looking up from his iPhone. "Marcy gets on my nerves, too. She's always whining about something. I told Renee to give her a little taste of her own medicine, see if she would shape up if we didn't cater to her."

Tom and Jose exchanged glances. "When did you talk to Renee?" Jose asked.

"Oh, I don't know—Tuesday, I guess," said Bob. "She was pretty upset after you talked to her and she wanted some feedback from me."

"Yeah, but Renee doesn't deal with any of your clients," said Tom. "I thought we agreed it'd be more efficient if we triaged human resource problems so that we didn't have overlap in these things?"

"Well, what was I supposed to say—I know I'm an officer of the company, but you're not on my agenda?"

Listen ... we cannot keep scheduling three-on-one meetings with every single employee on the payroll. It's ridiculous and it's a major waste of time.

Renee had been on the MTG payroll for 18 months, long enough to demonstrate that she was in no way the ideal customer service representative. She didn't have the knack of handling clients, especially if it involved dealing with administrative underlings rather than a firm's top person. Every time Jose talked with her about it, she managed to raise the issue with Bob, who somehow conveyed the idea that Renee was being put-upon not only by the client but by Jose, as well.

As a technician, Bob was great, thought Tom. As an administrator—well, if Tom had the proverbial dollar for every time Bob said "I'm an officer of the company," MTG's bottom line could be written in black, rather than red. The guy was relentless about reminding everyone that he was a partner. Not for the first time, Tom wished he had offered Bob double his salary, instead of the 15 percent ownership share.

"We've got a problem with Gene Barker, too," said Jose. "He totally screwed up the Spectacular Sunglasses move to their new offices."

"How so?" asked Tom.

"Well, the move was supposed to be completed on Wednesday. Gene had made all the arrangements and the phones were supposed to be working in the new offices Thursday. He gets a call from AT&T Wednesday afternoon that there'd been a delay; the phones wouldn't be operational until Friday at the earliest. Does he call Louis and let him know? No. He leaves a note on the door of the new offices.

"So instead of giving Louis the option of staying in the old office for two more days with operational phones, he lets a completely phone-centric company move into new offices with no telecommunications. Louis was screaming when he reached me. It's going to take a lot of stroking before his blood pressure comes down—if he didn't need us for the phones, I think he would have fired us on the spot. I thought we'd had Gene go through the customer training-philosophy thing. He manages to piss people off even when their systems work perfectly."

"I'll talk to him," said Bob. "I'll schedule a meeting for him to talk with the three of us."

"No!" Tom blurted out the word without thinking. He pushed away the second half of his sandwich. Jose was looking at his watch, gauging how much longer he could linger without being late for his next appointment.

"Listen," said Tom, "we cannot keep scheduling three-on-one meetings with every single employee on the payroll. It's ridiculous and it's a major waste of time. The three of us have to get it together and let everyone know that each one of us is going to tell them the exact same damn thing, so there's no point shopping around for a second opinion!

Geez, they play us like they're six-year-olds and we're mom and dad."

"I agree. But right now, I've gotta go," said Jose, rising with his tray.

"Yeah, me, too," said Bob. "And I won't be in tomorrow; it's parent-teacher conferences and Diane and I thought we'd get lunch together. She's been giving me grief about late nights, so I'm going to placate her with a little luxury shopping. I might try to get in a round of golf, too."

— The Classroom —

BREAKPOINT #1

Charting Your Course

We were both miserable.

Tom brought the class to attention, "I've asked my partner Jose to join us in this discussion," gesturing to a guest who had been silent until now.

"I thought Tom was going to blow a gasket over Bob's priorities," Jose told the class. More stout than Tom, Jose's dark hair was streaked with gray strands that emphasized unruly waves. As always, he was wearing a Polo shirt, jeans and running shoes.

"It's a good thing I was speechless," Tom told his graduate students. "I'm a scratch golfer—have been since high school. I hadn't played golf for six months! My wife and I hadn't been out to dinner, had people over or gone to a movie except for her birthday.

"We'd been in business—oh, I don't know—seven or eight years. We had plenty of clients, we had eight or nine employees, and our gross earnings were well into seven figures. We had a great reputation.

"But every time we turned around, it seemed like we had to have a meeting between the three of us. And I was miserable."

"We were both miserable," Jose said. "On paper, we looked like a very successful company, always ahead of the curve—

because we weren't focused on technology, we were focused on *solution*s and customer service."

"Behind the scenes, though, I was constantly juggling," said Tom. "The invoices, the bills, the complaints, the petty interactions that would come up between this technician and that client," said Tom. "I was totally stressed out."

"Bob and I were busting balls doing the technical work," added Jose, shaking his head at the memory. "We'd reached the point where it was taking us 63 days to collect on outstanding invoices! We were leveraging our credit cards every two weeks just to make payroll—and even then we weren't always sure we could do it."

We failed to make a plan. We didn't have processes that would deliver us to our destination.

"We didn't know it—we *wouldn't* know it for years, yet—but Jose and I had hit our first *BreakPoint*, the one that probably kills more businesses than any other," Tom said, taking over again.

"The thing is, this *BreakPoint* is like a rare disease. You can have it for years without recognizing it. You keep having symptoms, you treat them, you think you've beat the thing, you feel better for a while, but it keeps coming back in another form. It ain't going away 'til you get the right diagnosis.

"And that's not even the worst part," he said, shifting positions. "The worst part is, all those treatments can kill the business just as quickly—or more so—than the disease."

"So, what's the disease?" someone asked.

Tom let the silence linger. Finally he smiled. "The answer, my friends, is simple," he said. "We failed to make a plan. We didn't have processes that would deliver us to our destination. And we damn near didn't make it."

He paused another second, looked at the class and then repeated himself, more softly this time and without the smile, "We damn near didn't make it."

"And you know what?" Tom added. "If we start a new business tomorrow, we might make some of the same mistakes. But, because we've been through it before, we will—at least I hope we will—recognize and rectify them faster."

"That's today's cheat. You've got to have a *for real* plan ... and make sure you communicate it to others on the team ... over and over again.

A young woman raised her hand. "How can you have a plan," she asked, "when you don't know what it is you're planning for?"

"Are you talking a business plan, you know, financials and all that?" asked another student. "What could you two have done differently, in terms of planning, when you started MTG?"

"Great questions," said Jose. Tom nodded.

"We are talking about making a life plan, creating a vision of the life you want to lead," Jose added. "Only then can you create a business that will serve that plan."

Tom went to the board and wrote a list of questions. "Ask yourself these questions," he said, underlining phrases for emphasis:

What do I want my life to look like?

Why am I going into business for myself?

What do I want the business to accomplish or stand for?

What is my goal for the business, both in the immediate future and long-term?

How will the business allow me to lead the life I envision?

"We are not asking for philosophical essays to answer these questions," said Jose. The two had obviously discussed this point many times. "The answers may be no more than a sentence or two:

- I want the challenge of creating something of my own design. I enjoy risks and rewards—and I'm willing to put in the hours and all my resources to make it succeed.

- I want stability and security for my family, including financial comfort.

- I'm going into business because I can do what I do better than anyone is currently doing it—and I want my efforts to benefit my family first and foremost.

- I want to travel for a substantial part of every year and plan my work around my destination or schedule. I can do that, if I have my own business and I'm willing to trust in others.

"Planning is not a one-shot process. It's not about a 50-page business plan," said Tom. "It is about having a vision for your life and for your company, then using those as benchmarks for every strategic decision that has to be made. It is also about communicating the vision to every employee so they, too, know where the company is headed—and whether they're willing to go in that direction.

"Of course," Tom continued, "the plan must be flexible to allow for unexpected opportunities or emergencies. Some of those may lead the company in a new direction, some—even some of the ostensibly great opportunities—may threaten the stability of the business. The plan is one tool for evaluating the pros and cons of any decision, whether it be bringing on a new partner or offering a new service."

"Unfortunately, we've found that the way most people start a business," Jose interjected, "including Tom and me, is with the idea they will make more than they'll spend. When they inevitably come up against an obstacle outside their own experience, they don't ask for help. One key to on-the-job planning is to trust your instincts when something 'doesn't feel right' or you are in unfamiliar waters—and ask for help!"

"Planning is exploring all possibilities, to the extent reasonable, without falling into what we call 'paralysis by analysis,'" Tom concluded.

"Planning is being clear about what you want from life and how your business will get you there, analyzing your tolerance for risk and being honest about your ability to keep focused on your goals."

Tom went to the board and summarized the first *BreakPoint*:

BreakPoint #1: Charting the Course

• Decide the mission of your business.

• Decide what you want out of life and what you are willing to do—and to give up—to get it.

• Develop the road map to get there.

"That's it guys—see you next week," he said.

The MTG Story

*I'm not an entrepreneur, I'm just a technician
having an entrepreneurial seizure!*

The July air had pasted Tom's shirt to his back like wallpaper. Condensation on his bottle of beer dripped against his hand as he circulated through Shaw Park, chatting with existing and prospective clients. He spotted Jose across the patio and raised his bottle in greeting. These monthly Chamber-sponsored summer gatherings had proven useful for client networking, but also gave them the chance to mingle with business owners like themselves.

Jose was leaning in close to a balding man in his late fifties, a slender man with a longish nose and crinkles around his eyes—the look of a character actor perennially cast as the wise and wisecracking father in made-for-TV-movies. Tom recognized him as Donald Peters, executive director of a local medical services firm with a good reputation. He, Jose and Bob had heard Peters speak on the importance of business mentors and peer groups a few months earlier.

Tom had been impressed enough to find and join a regional IT group, as well as a local group with owners from several industries. The idea was to share experiences, good and bad, and trade advice. The first meeting had been an eye-opener. One member, a homebuilder, was in danger of losing his business—the firm had taken on a $1 million project that turned into a disaster. The others evaluated the problems and discussed how each of them could avoid the same missteps.

Tom headed toward the two men. "Hey, Don," Tom said, extending his hand. "How's the summer treating you?" They small-talked for a minute before Jose interrupted.

"I've been telling Don we've had a few problems with the business lately. He's got some good ideas we could try."

"A few problems?" thought Tom. "As in just squeaking by on payroll? Or relying on credit cards to cover expenses?" But he didn't say anything, just smiled uneasily and shifted his weight from side to side.

Don smiled, too. "It just wouldn't be a picnic without the ants, would it?" he said, which had the effect of putting Tom at ease.

"Don was telling me about a book he thinks would be helpful ... might give us some ideas about how to organize things to flow a little better," said Jose. "It's called *The E Myth, Revisted* by Michael Gerber. I'm going to get a copy." Tom recognized an enthusiasm he didn't often see in Jose. On impulse—or maybe, he thought later, instinct—he extended an invitation.

"Could you make time to meet with us for a couple of hours sometime soon?" he asked the older man. "I'm thinking we could use your advice."

What you need to be focusing on is creating the business. Leave the delivery aspects to your employees.

"I'd be glad to," Don responded. The three parted a few moments later, after entering an appointment for the following week in their respective PDAs. "In the meantime," said Tom, "I'll get The E Myth, too and give it a read."

"Wow! I couldn't believe how on-target this book was," Tom said, as he sat down in a restaurant booth with Don and Jose. He put an already dog-eared copy of *The E-Myth, Revisited* on the table, its pages fluttering with yellow Post-it notes.

"There was a description that fits me precisely—I'm not an entrepreneur, I'm just a technician having an entrepreneurial seizure! We're all good with our technical skills but not a damn one of us knows anything about running a business."

Don chuckled. "I see you've gotten Gerber's point: A good business owner works to make the business capable of running without its leader."

"Yeah," said Jose, who had brought along his own copy. "I liked the quote from Theodore Roosevelt—

The best executive is the one who has sense enough to pick good men to do what he wants done, and is self-reliant enough to keep from meddling with them while they do it!

You guys have been making a classic mistake," Don said, as they finished lunch and the conversation was winding down. "You've been concentrating on delivering MTG's services. What you need to be focusing on is creating the business. Leave the delivery aspects to your employees."

"But what if they screw it up?" Tom asked. "I don't want my clients to suffer because one of my people screws up—and it seems like they do—if I'm not there to back 'em up."

"Two questions," said Don. "First of all, how is anyone going to learn from their mistakes if you don't let them make mistakes and, when they do, you step in to fix them? More importantly, why aren't you hiring people so good that you trust them enough to fix their own mistakes?"

"Good questions," said Jose, as Tom nodded.

"That's your biggest challenge—the biggest challenge for any business," said Don.

"Hire the right people, talented people. Provide the right atmosphere for them to succeed. Then stand back and let them do their work delivering MTG's services. Your job is to recruit and hire those people, then keep them satisfied."

BREAKPOINT #2

Building Your Pit Crew

Everyone was their own boss, doing things their own way.

"What I hadn't learned was how to lead the team, how to pull it together and manage people, so that we worked like a machine instead of everyone doing their own thing at their own pace."

"We thought we were hiring good people but we were really just shopping for Band-Aids," Tom told the class. "We had never taken the time to consider what the problems really were."

"We kept trying to hire our way out of a crisis," said Jose, who was back in the classroom.

"Yeah, and every time we hired someone, I'd think, 'Well, that will take some of the pressure off'—but it never did," Tom added. "At one point, we brought on somebody whose sole job was to collect outstanding bills."

"But somehow," Jose finished, "she didn't put the same effort into it that an owner would."

The two talked almost as though they were back in those tension-filled days, the students momentarily forgotten.

"It was like everyone was their own boss, doing things their own way," Jose continued. "And I'm not talking doing just technical things their own way—every guy billed on his own schedule, wrote things up however he saw fit. We had Renee, who handled

43

some of the billing and another woman, Susan, who was really good working with the technicians.

"But it was like everything was off the menu—imagine going into a restaurant five nights a week and every time you went in, you had to ask the waitress what there was on the menu that night; how it was going to be cooked; who was the cook; what his mood was. Nothing was standardized. I may be exaggerating, but it seemed like we were starting from scratch every day."

Tom interjected. "I was feeling like it was a busy Saturday night—every night—at my father's restaurant when nobody showed up, not the cook, not the bartender, not the dishwasher.

"I had learned to do all those individual jobs at the restaurant," he continued. "What I hadn't learned was how to lead the team, how to pull it together and manage people so that we worked like a machine, instead of everyone doing their own thing at their own pace.

"If I could go back and change anything in the early years, it would be the concept of hiring more competent employees and delegating more effectively," Tom told the class. "I couldn't do it all by myself, and I couldn't solve every problem."

The business of the business owner is the business.

One of the grad students raised a hand: "Doesn't that seem pretty obvious?"

"Ya think?" Tom responded. "There were so many of these simple lessons that we hadn't learned. Plus, we were always responding to a crisis. It was, 'Get someone— anyone—in here fast to fix this problem!'"

He put his foot up on a chair and leaned an elbow on his knee. "In that first lunch, Don introduced me to three concepts that I'd never thought about—and remember, Don didn't have any technical expertise or experience in our field.

"The first is a little hard to grasp. But the gist is that my job was not to sell services. My job was to create and maintain the business, so that my employees could sell services."

He went to the white board and scrawled:

The business of the business owner is the business.

"It was fun to say that I owned my own business, but not knowing how to manage it took much of the joy out of it. I was very good at selling the product. Jose, Bob and their teams were great at satisfying clients. But none of us knew how to run a business. As I said, I'll get back to this topic later."

"Point two," he said, writing again:

Hire good people.

"I was an excellent sales person, the best in the company. But I learned that I needed to be the best recruiter.

"Recruiting is just like making a sale. You don't pitch the deal to new clients right off the bat. You talk, you court them, you develop a relationship. Maybe you don't even know they're potential clients, and they don't know it, either. Then one day—you realize you need each other.

"You need to recruit constantly. Hiring isn't like speed dating: bing, bang, boom and the deal is sealed. If you're serious about hiring the best people, you keep your eyes open *all the time*. So when you get an opening, you have a portfolio of prospects.

"The second part of hiring good people is knowing how to evaluate them. Develop a system. It never occurred to me that I could objectively measure the costs and benefits of hiring a particular person. That's something I'm sure is addressed in some of your other business classes."

He wrote on the board again:

Delegate.

"The third concept was: Delegate and give your employees the freedom to do their jobs, even if they make a mistake and have to fix it once in a while. This was really hard for me.

"I never wanted anyone to make a mistake and when they did, I would rail at them so much they eventually didn't want to make any decisions at all, for fear that I would overrule them or they would be wrong. It took me a long time to remember that I learn best when I make mistakes—but I never took that lesson to the business.

"But I don't want to get ahead of myself. You can't delegate until you've hired the right people, great people."

Tom paused and looked at his students. "Anyone see a problem with this?" No one responded. He gestured at one of them.

"Jack, say I come to you—I'm the owner of a fledgling business and you have been working in a related industry for six or seven years—I come to you and say, 'Hey, Jack, I've heard great things about you, you're tops in your field. I'd like you to come on board with us. We can't pay you as much as you're making and the company isn't fully established, but we'd really like to have you on our team.' Whaddya say, Jack?"

Jack thought, then shook his head. "Why would I do that—I'm already established. If I want a better job, I can probably go out and get one that pays me more, not less.

Plus, in this economy, I'm looking for a little job security."

"Exactly!" said Tom.

"That's one of the difficulties for small businesses. It can be very hard to hire really good people when you can't offer strong incentives to lure them from their current jobs. What that means is the business owner sometimes has to settle for a less-than-perfect fit—I think it's pretty clear that Bob, for example, was not a good fit, at least not as a partner.

"What it doesn't mean is that you have to settle for someone who is ineffective or a really bad fit. For me, the key is to find someone, first of all, with the education and ability to do the job. Experience is great, but you can't always afford it.

"The key is what Don calls the 'three-legged-stool strategy.' A stool needs three legs for stability. They can't be randomly spaced—the support has to be balanced.

"Same thing goes for a company. Everyone has their strengths and their weaknesses; nobody's perfect. What you look for is someone strong in the area where you or your existing team is weak.

"Take Bob as an example. He was strong in the same area, technical expertise, as Jose. He was weak in administrative skills, which is what both Jose and I were lacking. It was like adding the third leg to a stool right next to one of the other legs. What happens? The stool falls over.

"We'll talk later about how to overcome this difficulty," he said. "But for now, remember this: Failure to hire good people or failing to give them authority and responsibility to do their jobs—even if it means they make mistakes—is one of the *Break-Points* at which many companies fail."

The MTG Story

*"Right now, we're nothing but small fry—and no one is
ever going to want to buy us if we're just small fry."*

Neither Tom nor Jose had thought to invite Bob to the lunch
with Don. Tom had considered the meeting just an informal
conversation, but as they talked with Don, Tom wished he
had invited their third partner. Because he had gotten it into
his head—and he was sure Jose would agree—that MTG
should hire this guy.

Don didn't have technical expertise. But he did have
just what MTG needed at the moment—years of experience
structuring a business in a way that allowed orderly growth.
He'd worked at a number of businesses around town, the last
eight for a business that had grown from a one-man start-up
to about 40 employees.

Jose did agree that Don would bring something important
to MTG. Bob emphatically did not. This was a pattern, Tom
reflected, that kept recurring. He and Jose seemed to agree
easily on almost every decision while Bob inevitably needed
coaxing. Tom realized a large part of Bob's resistance in this
case stemmed from his knowledge that the other two partners
had met with Don alone.

"Yeah, we should have had him come along," Tom acknowledged to himself. At the same time, he was irritated at the
effort it took to placate Bob—who kept reminding Tom that
"I'm a partner, I should have been there."

Once again, Tom fervently wished for a do-over on that
decision. And much as he hated to admit it, Bob was right—

MTG didn't have the money to hire Don. Tom knew it, Jose knew it and Don knew it. Tom looked at the books every which way he could, but there was no blood to be wrung out of the ledgers.

He and Don had lunch a week after the argument with Bob.

"I know you'd be great for getting us on the right track," he told Don, "I just can't see any way of making it work financially."

"Listen, Tom. I know I'd be right for you, too, and I think I can help you make it work," Don said. "Here's the deal."

"My kids are through college. I got out of the stock market before the bubble blew and the mortgage is about done. So I'm open to creative financing ..."

Tom's eyebrows came together. "Like what?"

"Like we come up with some parameters for measuring what benefit I bring you—increased sales, reduction in debt load, decrease in outstanding receivables—and we set up a compensation plan based on the results ..."

"Like deferred billing or something?" Tom asked.

"Deferred compensation," Don replied, "probably in the form of stock options or a share of equity. Talk it over with Jose—and God forbid, don't forget Bob—and see if you're interested. I'll shoot some numbers and ideas over to you."

Tom nodded. "Don, that would be great. I don't know how to thank you ..."

Don held up his hand. "Oh, I'm not doing it for you," he said, smiling. "I'm doing it for me. I'm ready for a new challenge—and the idea of more golf just bores me to tears."

It took a while, but Tom—exercising all the diplomacy

and restraint he could muster—got Bob to agree to hiring Don.

MTG was in trouble, more than Tom wanted to admit. The homebuilder in his peer group wasn't the only one with a "big opportunity" turning to dust.

He and Bob were wrangling over money—again. Jose, as usual, was staying above the fray. Whenever the three were together lately, Tom seethed, Bob wore the expression of a sullen teenager and Jose, if he spoke at all, made conciliatory small talk.

One big issue was investment. Jose's business management software linking electronic records—budgets, sales figures, leading indicators—into a dashboard easily adaptable to different operating systems was ready for prime time. Tom was on the verge of closing a multi-year deal with a company hot for the software. The drawback?

The partners had to put up $30,000, in amounts equal to their ownership shares, to complete the legal work necessary to bring the program to market. That meant Bob had to contribute $4,500. He absolutely refused.

"That's what a partnership is—you kick in your share of costs, you don't just get to reap the benefits," Tom said in one heated meeting between the three of them. "If we want to build this company, we've all got to make an investment."

"That's not what I signed on for, and my wife sure as hell didn't sign on for it, either," Bob shouted back. "Either we grow the company with what the company has in the bank— or we don't grow it. I don't have that kind of cash to throw around. I think MTG is fine as it is. Who says we have to get bigger, anyway?"

"I say so," Tom shot back. "The whole point, if we're ever going to make big money is to 'be' big. Right now, we're nothing but small fry—and no one is ever going to want to buy us if we're just small fry."

It was the first time Tom had articulated to himself that his ultimate goal was to grow the company and sell it. He was a little surprised by the realization, but it was true. And Jose's software would be a big selling point. It had to be developed.

"Jose, where do you stand?" Tom asked. He hated to put Jose on the spot but damn it, Jose had to take a stand once in a while. And Jose had already told Tom he had the cash reserves and he agreed it was time to put the money on the line.

"I've thought it through and I have to say, Bob, I agree with Tom." Jose spoke deliberately, almost anxiously. "If we skimp on the resources, we're going to have a shoddy product. I wouldn't want to put out anything that wasn't great."

"What about growth, why do we have to grow?" Bob countered. "Why do we have to grow and sell?"

"Well," said Jose, "even if we don't sell, we still have to get bigger. Otherwise, what's the point in having our own business—right now we work longer hours than we would for anyone else and we don't take home all that much more money."

The issue simmered until Bob agreed to put up $1,500 and take a no-interest loan for the rest from Tom and Jose. The atmosphere remained sour for months, especially when it became clear they needed more people—and no one wanted to bring it up, because it would mean more arguments over money.

Don spent his first week observing operations. Which wasn't all that difficult considering there were just 13 employees. He called a meeting with the partners for the following Tuesday.

"Well," he said. "I'm impressed with your dedication to customer service. It's obviously a key part of your success."

Before the partners could congratulate themselves, Don continued. "But I'm amazed you've gotten this far without a leadership structure—it's like you're climbing a mountain of spaghetti. You're damn lucky you haven't rolled off the mountain like meatballs."

Tom and Jose shifted uncomfortably in their chairs. Bob sat back and crossed his arms across his chest, eyes narrowed.

"Really, guys," said Don, relaxed and casual in an open-necked sports shirt. "This ain't high school and you ain't the second-string football team. You've got a good shot at being first string—but only if you get yourself a quarterback. In fact, it's like you've been playing touch football in the NFL. So far, you've been lucky but that could change at any moment, unless you wake up and smell the coffee."

Don, the others soon realized, had a way of mixing metaphors but getting his points across anyway.

... You have got to get together on what it is you want to build, and pick which one is going to be the lead contractor. Then get your systems and processes in place to get the building done.

"This business of the three of you signing off on every decision is a waste of time, not to mention that the three of you don't even come to consensus when you do meet. Half the time, you're not only NOT on the same page—you aren't even reading the same book. Somebody's got to be top dog.

"Second, if you three are the meatballs, the rest of the organization is the bowl of spaghetti, all tangled up in the sauce. That's a great Italian dinner, but it's no way to run a business."

"I thought you said the first key to success is hiring good people and delegating," said Tom.

"Yeah, I did say that," Don responded. "But before you can do that, you have to have a clear idea of what you want them to do once they are hired. And you need a clear process for hiring—and someone authorized to make the hires—so that the three of you aren't all wrapped up in the process."

He paused a second. "Process. Now there's a concept I think you all should get to know. It makes life so much simpler!" He chuckled, to soften the criticism.

"Process is like the bone structure of a building. Once you've got a skeleton, it's easier to make decisions on what to do next—do you need to put in more bathrooms, do you need a parking garage, is there room for a cafeteria? Right now it looks like you're adding elevators before you've got a working heating system or electrical grid.

"In fact, I'd say you've been slapping together a tool shed with the hope of turning it into a shopping center."

Don paused and drank from his ever-present can of Dr. Pepper. Tom went to the small refrigerator under the credenza in the meeting room, took a soda for himself and tossed one to Bob. Jose waved away the offer of a Diet Coke. The three partners took the brief break as an opportunity to digest what Don had already said.

"It sounds like you want us to go back to Square One," Bob said. "Isn't that going to set revenues and growth back, too?"

"Listen, guys," Don said. "You do need to go back to Square One—and it's going to make life so much easier and more productive. Right now, you keep going to clients over and over to fix the same problems, but you never resolve the underlying issues ..."

"Like what?" Bob asked.

"Like knowing when a job is completed, when it should be billed and how soon you should be collecting," said Don.

"Right now, every member of your technical team— including you two," he said, gesturing toward Jose and Bob, "is using an individual system. The financial administrator doesn't get timely information, so she can never get the invoices out in a timely way. When clients get a late bill, they question it because the work isn't fresh in their mind— and their questions delay payment even more. Am I right?"

The three partners exchanged glances and nodded.

"What you'll find out is that, when you capture the work and bill it right away, clients ask fewer questions and pay faster. You know what that means? It means you won't be leveraging your credit cards to make payroll. Processes, my friends, processes!"

He took another sip.

"Listen, the three of you have got to get together on what it is you want to build, and pick which one is going to be the lead contractor. Then get your systems and processes in place to get the building done.

"MTG is still in the stage where this won't be difficult. This is where hiring the right people—with the right skills—is essential. Hire someone with billing experience and that person can set up the billing process. And that process will be standardized, not something you, or whomever you happened to tap, makes up because it works for the moment.

"Believe me, getting people with experience who can implement systems for you will make life easier now, when there are fewer than a dozen employees who have been muddling along. When—if—MTG gets bigger, having these systems in place will be essential to your success."

Tom and Jose and even Bob were nodding their heads, though all three looked slightly befuddled—as though they hadn't yet fully absorbed Don's message. He finished his Dr. Pepper and added a final thought.

"Right now, this company is like a man in New York determined to get to Los Angeles without any idea of why he wants to go, where it is or what the options are for getting there. He could have a long walk ahead of him if he hasn't realized there's an airport nearby."

— *The Classroom* —

"I was finally beginning to develop a plan."

"In a week, Don put his finger on something Jose, Bob and I hadn't figured out in eight years," said Tom. "It's almost unbelievable, but in our defense, the company was growing so fast we didn't have time—or we didn't make time—to step back and see what was happening.

"Plus, we didn't really think of ourselves as businessmen, at least Jose and I didn't. We had the mindset of buddies who had gone into business, almost like a couple of kids who decided to wash cars during the summer. We ran things on kind of a loosey goosey basis—we'd agree that such-and-such a decision would be up to the lead technician on a particular job and the project coordinator assigned to that technician. But in the end, we three would have to have a meeting to approve the simplest things.

"Don taught me that running a business requires a totally different skill set than selling or delivering our services. This was his first big lesson for me.

When you start working "on the business,"
you start to plan what you want the business to
accomplish and what it will look like in the future.

"He also taught me how to work 'on the business,' rather than 'in the business,' which is what we had been doing since the beginning."

A student raised her hand. "What's the difference?" she asked.

"Good question," Tom said. "I would define working 'in the business' as focusing on day-to-day tactical issues that need to get addressed. It's a very reactive way to operate and one that feels out of control. It means the business goes wherever it's going, without any direction or purpose.

"When you start working 'on the business,' you start to plan what you want the business to accomplish and what it will look like in the future. You also start examining where you spend your time, what processes you've got in place and whether you have the right mix of clients. This is a proactive approach. It makes running a business a hell of a lot more effective—and more fun, too."

"Like I said, until Don came along, we hadn't done any of those things. And just getting our minds around the concepts took us a while."

He stood and stretched.

Tom added a quick caveat. "The CEO is like the chief engineer. He's involved to the extent that he's sure the various parts of the machine are running smoothly. But he shouldn't be applying oil to this cog or adjusting the springs on the undercarriage—he leaves that to his department heads. That's what Don meant by working on the business, not in it."

"So how did you decide who was going to be CEO," asked a young man, his fingers poised over his keyboard to capture the answer.

"We flipped coins," Tom said, drawing a few gasps from the group.

"NOT!" That was a big bone of contention. Jose was very open to me becoming CEO, but Bob wasn't. He believed he could manage the business better than any of us—and if I had agreed with him, I would have considered letting him do it.

"But I didn't believe that. More important, I started to realize that Bob had a different picture of the business than I had in mind. His approach wasn't bad, it just didn't fit with the goals I was developing."

He paused a second. "See," he said. "I was finally beginning to develop a plan. And I was learning about hiring well and then letting those top-notch people do their jobs.

"Despite our best efforts to screw things up, we were clawing our way over the first two *BreakPoints*."

Tom went to the white board and summarized his second *BreakPoint*:

BreakPoint #2: Building Your Pit Crew

• **Recruit the best.**

• **Invest in the hiring process.**

• **Let people do their jobs within the structure you've created.**

"So guys, see you next week …"

The MTG Story

You can really understand why you get along or don't, and how you can be more effective working with one another.

Tom was hyped as he blew into MTG's conference room for the partners' weekly meeting with Don. He began as soon as all four had settled around the table.

"We've got to give this thing called DISC a try," he said. "This woman, Jo Murphy, is incredible at evaluating the results and I think it could really be great for the company."

Neither Bob nor Jose had the faintest idea what he was talking about. Don seemed bemused.

"What's a DISC evaluation?" Jose asked.

"What's it going to cost us?" Bob interjected.

"Why do we need it?" added Jose.

"Listen," said Tom. "Basically, it's a tool for evaluating a person's communication style and values, what they want out of life and how that affects what they do at work. It sounds like voodoo, but it's not—it's a great tool for evaluating what motivates a particular person and assessing how he or she fits into the organization."

"I'm familiar with DISC—there are a lot of behavior assessment tools out there," said Don. "I don't know Jo Murphy. I have to tell you, I've never been that impressed with these things to run an organization. But Tom, tell us what you know."

Tom grinned, only a little abashed by his own enthusiasm. "The IT peer group I joined a few months ago had us all take this online survey of our behavior patterns. Then Jo Murphy—she's a consultant from out of town—evaluated our results.

She came in and explained why the results are relevant to business. Everyone agreed she was spot-on describing people's motivations and management style.

"It was like having a good psychologist help you understand what motivates you, how you get things done, what your communication style is and how you take in information and make decisions.

"But that's not the point," he went on. "That's just when the real work begins—when you learn how to use the results to communicate better with the people you work with. You can really understand why you get along or don't, and how you can be more effective working with one another."

"Sounds like a shrink," said Bob. Jose nodded. Even Don looked skeptical; for once, the three were in agreement.

"Here's how much I believe in it," Tom said. "I had Amanda take the DISC, and Jo evaluated the results. "Amanda and I ended up talking about the differences in our styles and how we perceive what we're saying to each other. We're already communicating so much more clearly—and I thought we were really communicating well before we did this."

"I'm so happy for the two of you," said Jose, needling his friend a little. "But I ask again: Why does MTG need this?"

"Listen, it all fits into the bigger picture—a philosophy of open communication, where everyone feels free to speak up and contribute in the best interest of the company," Tom said. "I think this could smooth out some rough spots we've had. What can it hurt to have her come in and give a presentation? Our only cost would be a plane ticket and a nice lunch."

Jose didn't seem to care, one way or another. Don shrugged his shoulders, and Bob grumbled a little about the cost. After a bit more push from Tom, they agreed to bring Jo Murphy to the office and give this DISC thing a try.

"So, do you know everything about me?" Tom asked Jo Murphy after greeting her. She laughed, shook her head and said something non-committal but comforting—which led Tom to believe that she might, indeed, know quite a lot about him. He thought that realization should make him nervous but Jo's demeanor put him at ease. "Well," he said, "let's get to the conference room and get started."

If Don, Bob and Jose were expecting a high-powered no-nonsense executive type in a suit and high heels, they were surprised by Jo Murphy. She was wearing a blue-skirted suit and low pumps but she came across as more girlish or motherly than high-powered. Small, mid-fortyish and slightly plump, she had a firm handshake and dimples. If she was wearing makeup at all, it was only a trace of lipstick.

She was there to debrief all four men on their DISC assessments, first as a group and then individually. Jo handed each of them a 50-page report, including graphs charting their own characteristics. She also gave each the cover sheet from the others' evaluations, so all four could see the general results.

"What's the point of knowing all this, especially about other people?" Bob asked.

"Good question," said Jo. "These things are not about personality, skills or intelligence. This is about understanding behavior. The goal is to know a person's strengths, to take advantage of them. Knowing a person's weaker points—how he responds under stress—makes it easier to communicate or mitigate the weak points. It can also make it easier to place people in positions that are right for them."

Seeing that the partners still look confused, Jo turned to Don. "Take Don, for example. I'm not going to go into all the ins-and-outs of the results, but his natural style makes him an excellent administrator. He's a process guy, he's task-oriented and utilitarian. Don's satisfaction comes in seeing things working and keeping them working. He doesn't feel the need to take a lot of risks or claim a lot of glory."

Don raised his eyebrows and nodded slightly, as if to acknowledge her accuracy.

"And how does that help the company," Bob persisted.

When you understand your own behavior—and how it affects others—and your partner's behavior, then you can adjust for the differences. You end up playing up the strengths, not the weaknesses.

"Here's how," Jo responded. "If one member of a management team is basically hard-driving, big-picture oriented with maybe a short attention span—a dynamic, go-go-go type, and another partner is just as smart but much more oriented to detail, maybe more reflective and slower to come to conclusions because he needs data while the first partner goes more on intuition, they might make a really complementary team.

"They could also totally mess up their business through miscommunication. The first partner gets impatient with the second one, waiting for an opinion. He presses for a decision. This makes the second partner anxious and he pulls back, because he's really thinking about the facts. They're both misinterpreting the actions of the other, 'cause neither one understands the way the other partner processes information.

"Worse, neither one realizes how he is coming across. The go-go-go guy doesn't see himself as a bully or arrogant and the data-oriented partner doesn't see himself as indecisive or unwilling to take a stand. But that's how they see one another.

"When you understand your own behavior—and how it affects others—and your partner's behavior, then you can adjust for the differences. You end up playing up the strengths, not the weaknesses.

"Nobody is all of one thing and none of the others," she reminded them. "Everyone is a mix of behaviors and motivations."

"I'm exhausted already," said Jose. "Let's take a break."

— The Classroom —

BREAKPOINT #3
Communicating on Purpose

*"I clearly understood, for the first time,
that not everyone functions the way I do."*

Tom turned to the woman sitting in the chair next to him, a woman with elfish brown eyes, and introduced her to the class.

"This is Jo Murphy. I count her as one of my angels—working with Jo accelerated MTG's success by about a thousand-fold," he said. "She's going to tell you a little bit more about why creating a culture of communication—and a language that everyone in the company understands—is so important."

Tom had already given a brief explanation of the DISC evaluation, so one student was ready with a question even before Jo began.

"Is this like a Briggs-Meyers test?" he asked.

"Meyers-Briggs, actually. And, yes, it's similar in that it reveals an individual's motivations and behaviors," Jo replied. "But the results of all those tests are just tools—the main idea is to use what you learn to communicate more effectively with one another. That's the real work—using the tools to build your communication skills and the skills of your leadership team. It's like buying a new food processor or fancy oven. Just because you have one, doesn't make you a better cook. You still have to acquire and practice the skills to use them."

65

Tom broke in. "It was a whole process at MTG, getting to know ourselves and one another and *working* at opening up communications. The biggest takeaway for me? I clearly understood for the first time that not everyone functions the way I do."

"I don't understand what difference that makes," said a young woman. Jo took over again.

"Just to give you an example," she said, "I'm going to talk a little bit about Tom and Jose. They've always been good partners, but there was still some tension between them, especially if Jose didn't speak up to support one of Tom's decisions in an argument with Bob."

Tom nodded and Jo continued.

"Tom has no problem with conflict. He says what he thinks and he'll argue for his position. He's a fast thinker; he wants to get on with things.

"Jose, on the other hand, is much more fact-and process-oriented when it comes to making decisions. Tom always has a dozen things on his mind. Jose likes to think things through one at time."

Tom interrupted.

"I was getting enraged watching Jose during these arguments with Bob. He would sit quietly, never showing any concern or emotion," he said. "He seemed very distant and cold. I questioned whether he cared about the urgency of the issue.

"Once Jo explained the difference in our styles, I could see why Jose never felt comfortable challenging me. It also made sense that he didn't want to speak up when Bob and I were arguing. He was processing the facts. I was working on the same facts, but arguing on my intuition. But to Jose and Bob, it seemed like I was just insisting on my own point of view.

"This was a real epiphany for me. I never saw myself as a bully or even being 'in your face.'"

Not everyone functions the way I do; others see the world through a different lens.

"What Jo helped me figure out is, sometimes I need to sit back and listen—even when I know I'm right! Okay, just kidding. But seriously, I have to go through the discomfort of shutting up so that other people can take the time to develop and contribute their opinion."

"What that allowed Tom's partners to do," said Jo, "is ask him to slow down, to explain what he was thinking. Knowing his style made them less reluctant to challenge him. They could express their opinions.

"Tom, on the other hand, first of all recognized that he wasn't making himself clear. Knowing how the others operate also made him realize that they were asking him to communicate on their terms—they weren't disinterested or dumb or hostile. In other words, to use a kitchen analogy, these three guys had different ideas about how to make an omelet—and Tom had to let each of them make their breakfast eggs their own way, rather than insisting on his recipe."

"I realized that when someone questions my decision or has a different opinion, it's not personal," Tom said. "They are questioning because all of us have the best interest of the company uppermost in our minds. That alone made my communication with Jose—which had always been pretty good, as far as I was concerned—better.

"It even helped me deal with Bob. Knowing his underlying motives—which weren't bad, just different—helped me listen a *little* better without getting my back up when he opened his mouth. I had to believe he had the company's best interest at heart, too."

Jo broke in. "Tom didn't have any idea that how he made decisions or came across to others was as something of a bully— even to Jose, one of his closest friends. As far as Tom was concerned, it was Jose who wasn't speaking up or making a decision. It's like the worst kind of marriage miscommunication—one partner always thinks if he or she could just get the other one to change, their problems would disappear. To be fair, Jose had no idea either, why he wasn't speaking up or why Tom's decision-making sometimes made him so uncomfortable. That's why it's so important to look at yourself in the mirror, before you start judging how other people are acting."

"That *one* concept—that not everyone functions the way I do, that they see the world through a different lens," Tom said, "helped me develop as a leader more than anything."

The MTG Story

Tom thought his head would explode if Rachel Thompson didn't quit talking. He reminded himself that he should keep quiet so others could contribute. But Rachel had been complaining for 20 minutes about the sales department's non-compliance with MTG's project management processes—a topic relevant to three of the seven managers at the meeting. The rest were in a stupor.

What did Rachel not understand about "Be brief, be bright and be gone," the mantra Tom constantly invoked as the guidelines for these weekly sessions? "Rachel," he said, in his third attempt to close her down, "This is something you and I should talk about later. Right now, we need to move on."

Miffed, she sat down.

Rachel's obsessive attention to detail was both her strength and her weakness. She never let a project move off track, but she never yielded an iota on process, either.

Not a week went by that someone in sales—and even some clients—didn't complain about her stringent requirements. Rachel's skills had contributed a lot to MTG's growth but, after five years, the word "flexibility" was still not in her vocabulary.

And Rachel wasn't the only reason meetings ran long. Regardless of the agenda, there were always topics either over-discussed or, paradoxically, left uncovered. Even Jose lamented the waste of time. Tom pulled his attention back to the meeting long enough to bring it to a close.

"Another two hours shot to hell," he was saying the following Saturday, recounting the meeting to his golf partners. "These meetings take on a life of their own." The three of them played the Forest Park course monthly. Paul Green had taken his company public after building it from scratch to 600 employees. Paul was Tom's first business mentor. Rick Schwartz was a friend and occasional paid consultant to MTG.

Rick and Tom watched quietly as Paul sunk his putt for a birdie on the eighth hole.

"Tom, haven't you heard of the rhythm method?" Paul asked, retrieving his ball. Rick groaned and Tom looked startled. "The rhythm method of meetings," said Paul, repeating an oft-used old joke.

"Seriously, MTG is too big for gang meetings. They eat time, they frustrate everyone and nothing gets accomplished. You've got to break 'em down."

"It's true," Rick agreed, choosing a driver for the ninth hole. "You have to triage—what's immediate, what can hold and what's long-term."

"How do you mean?" Tom asked.

"How long are your weekly meetings?" Paul countered.

"Supposedly, 45 minutes," Tom responded. "Usually more like an hour-and-a-half or two hours."

"And what's the point?" Rick asked.

"You know—look at billings, what the problems are, how sales look for the next month, long-term projects or planning."

"*Waaaay* too much," said Paul, as they headed for the ninth hole.

"Yeah, like a bad stew with too many ingredients," added Rick.

"Who said that—it sounds familiar," Paul asked.

"Lencioni," Rick said. *Death by Meeting*.

— *The Classroom* —

Death by Meeting

Internal communications are complicated, more like a system or a spider web than a straight line.

Tom scrawled *Death by Meeting*, on the whiteboard, followed by the author's name, Patrick Lencioni.

"It's a great book, same guy that wrote *The Five Dysfunctions of a Team*, he said, turning to the class. "As Lencioni says, good meetings are passionate, unfiltered, messy and provocative. They speed decision making and wipe out the need to revisit issues again and again.

"Long story short, we adopted a version of Lencioni's meeting process,"

Tom said. "We developed what I call a *meeting rhythm*.

"Mondays, we have our weekly tactical meeting. We talk about the financials, sales projections for the next 30 days and work in progress. They last about 45 minutes. It's bing-bam-boom because everyone knows what to expect.

"This is where open communication comes in. Everyone is expected to give an opinion—no passes. Disagreements aren't personal. We don't recognize turf boundaries."

He guzzled half his bottle of water.

"The second meeting is monthly. It's more strategic, more long-term. It takes half a day. We look at developing issues— new directions in technology, stuff like that. If these things come up in the weekly meetings, someone says, 'Hey, let's park it.'

72

"The third meeting is twice-yearly and off-site," Tom continued. "It lasts two days and we talk about big challenges—new vendors, long-term planning, blue-sky visions for the company. And we have some of those infamous 'bonding' exercises led by consultants. We get to know one another, eat meals together. This is a time to see each other as people, not just business associates. It's an opportunity to build trust while we draw up our long-term plans.

"Adjusting the meeting schedules was great—it did make us more efficient and the off-site meetings did help us as leaders. But that was still just another phase in learning to communicate better.

"Remember the company newsletter I told you about? It was filled with information. Guess what? Nobody—well, almost nobody—read it. Turns out that employees—not just MTG's employees, everybody's employees, the world over—want to get company news, good or bad, face-to-face from their supervisor or manager."

A student raised her hand. "How about getting the information directly from the CEO, like in a town meeting?" she asked. "Isn't that better?"

"Yeah, we did that, too. And it was good. But still, people want to hear from their supervisor. That's the person they know and that's the person they figure can relate what's happening to the day-to-day operations. That's the person they expect to be able to get answers about what's going on in the company. And giving that person responsibility to communicate also gives him—or her—power.

"Internal communications are complicated, more like a system or a spider web than a straight line. And that's where we used Jo again. She took the communication training down to the next level, so that we could build a second-tier leadership team. Sharing information is good, but we were learning to share the power of sharing information."

Tom raised his arms above his head in a gesture that implied rather than said, "I know! I know!"

"It sounds convoluted. But think of it like plumbing—the hot water heater being the executive committee, the sinks and bathtubs being the working units. The water has to flow through the system and come out the faucets or shower heads. It lends a certain predictability to the plumbing, doesn't it?"

Ignoring a few groans from the students, Tom continued.

"But here's the thing. You do have to make damn sure the hot water is there when it's supposed to be. What I mean is, the company message has to be clear. To push my example, the hot water can't be picking up rust or sludge as it travels the pipes to the shower head. Anyone here ever turned on the water after it's been out of service for a few days and you get that sputtering, then brown water bubbles out for a while, before it turns clear?

If there is one thing I learned, it's that communication is not just talking.

"No matter how clearly you think you've conveyed your message, you have to keep checking to make sure it's actually been heard the way you meant it."

"So you don't play the telephone game?" asked a young man. "You know, whispering something down a line of people and it comes out garbled?"

"Exactly," Tom said.

"I saw this news report last weekend, about kids learning not to get into cars with strangers," said another student. "This elementary school brought in police officers to teach the "stranger danger" lesson—you know, run away from strangers, even if they tell you they need help finding a lost puppy?"

"Yeah," said a third student. "I saw it, too. Two days later, they had an undercover police officer pull up to these same kids and ask for help finding a puppy—three of the five kids he approached got into the car."

"Exactly," Tom said again. "It's not enough to say something once. You have to embed your message constantly and then ask for feedback to make sure it got through. 'Uh-huh,' does not count as an affirmative answer to 'Did you understand what I said?'"

He looked at his watch, signaling the end of class.

"I wish I could tell you that we'd solved all our communication problems at this point, but we hadn't. We really hadn't even addressed how to put our messages into action internally. That's a whole lesson in itself, turning the 'mission statement' into policy and then into practice. Internal communication is a constant process.

"If there is one thing I learned, it's that communication is not just talking.

You have to find a way to turn your values, your message, into action. Your people have to feel like they've got skin in the game of your business—and it's not just the fact they are getting a salary. The same thing goes for communicating your values to your partners, your customers, the community.

"It would be so great if you could deal with each one of these issues individually, one at a time. But you can't. What you have to do is just keep coping. Keep trying to understand what's happening, keep talking to one another. The best indicator of a company's chances of success, in my mind, is the ability of its leaders to keep learning—call on your mentors, read what you can and slog on through the mudflats.

"See you all next week."

The MTG Story

*Everyone should say how he or she feels, without being
afraid of looking foolish for raising valid questions.*

Jo started her third monthly meeting at MTG with a hug for
each man, then enthused over pictures of Jose's newborn and
asked Tom how his daughter was coping with a new school.
Bob and Don each received glowing smiles and an extra
squeeze with the hug.

Still flashing her dimples, Jo turned to Tom. "Anything
new?" All four knew Tom would be bursting with insights
learned since their last meeting. The concepts he'd learned
from Jo had turned on the proverbial light bulb over his head.

"I'll tell you one thing I learned about myself," he said.
"When I state my opinions, other people assume I'm stating
facts because I have confidence in everything I say. My wife
can't stand that, but now she's beginning to call me on it. I
never realized people were giving me that much credit."

Don and Jose immediately exchanged glances and rolled
their eyes.

"What?" asked Tom, grinning.

"Anyway, I get it that if everyone acted like me, we'd always
be starting something new and never finishing anything. That's
why Jose is such a good balance—he makes sure everything
gets done and done right.

"And I think we're communicating more clearly, don't
you?" he asked his partners. "Having different styles makes
us a more balanced team and helps us make better decisions."

> *If you are going to open the channels, you have to make sure everyone in the company—top to bottom—understands you are committed to a culture of candor.*

Jo turned to Jose, merely giving him a glance.

"We are asking better questions and it seems like we're getting to core issues faster, instead of just solving the surface problems," Jose said.

"Bob, what about you?" she asked.

Jo and Bob had met privately more than once. When she pointed out results on his DISC indicated an aversion to risk, Bob became defensive. "I left a stable job to join this company—that's a huge risk right there," he fumed. "But no, I didn't sign on with the plan of devoting my financial future to Tom's dreams."

He had no intention of discussing that or anything else with the others. So he merely rolled his eyes at Jo's question. After a few minutes of coaxing, she moved down the agenda.

"At this point, it's time for you to decide how to take this concept of open communication company-wide—if that's what you want. If you are going to open the channels, you have to make sure everyone in the company—top to bottom— understands you are committed to a culture of candor."

Bob heaved a sigh so obviously critical that Jo had no choice but to interrupt her presentation.

"Bob," she said, with her sweetest smile, "if you want to

disagree with something, the most appropriate way is to speak up and say 'I disagree.' That's what I mean by candor."

All four men froze. Tom caught one of Jose's enigmatic looks. Even Don seemed startled. Jo Murphy rarely said anything negative. But, in fact, Tom reflected, her comment hadn't been critical—just to the point. Bob's expression flashed from embarrassed to defiant to sheepish. Jo waited.

"I just think this is a bunch of touchy-feely bullshit," he said finally. "And how much is it going to cost to take this program to everyone in MTG?"

"Bob, congratulations," Jo said. "That is exactly the point. Everyone should say how he or she feels, without being afraid of looking foolish for raising valid questions. Otherwise, no one knows what the issues are until they reach a boiling point. That would not be in the best interests of the organization."

— *The Classroom* —

A Breakthrough

This was not a short-term deal.

"This was pretty big," Tom told the class when it met again. "And it was a real breakthrough. Bob *never* would have said anything so direct. He would just roll his eyes, which pissed me off and pretty soon, we'd be arguing.

"Not that we immediately agreed on spending the money to push this communication concept down the ranks. Bob, of course, was against it. I thought it would add value. But at least we didn't argue—or not as much as we would have before."

"So Bob got on board with the program?" asked one of the students.

Tom took a swig from his bottle of water.

"Well, not exactly," he admitted, drawing chuckles from the class. "I guess it wasn't so much a breakthrough as a good example of what Jo was trying to teach us. And how direct we were going to have to be in teaching everyone else."

"What do you mean," a student asked.

"We had to learn to actually communicate to one another, regardless of the difficulties," Tom replied. "If you don't speak up, no one knows what you are thinking—and what you are thinking might be perfectly valid. And if you don't speak up, you end up just building up resentment. So once we realized we had to be open with one another, then we had to figure out how to communicate to everyone else at MTG."

"How did you reach out to the rest of the company?" a student asked.

"This was not a short-term deal," Tom told his grad students. "We worked with Jo, on and off, for six years. We had a lot going on, restructuring the management team, building up business, looking for a sales manager. We used Jo's techniques to make things go more smoothly—especially in evaluating new people for our teams. This was a whole process, getting to know ourselves and one another and really *working* at opening up communications.

"We were trying to figure out how to communicate, what to communicate and who we were supposed to be communicating with. We started an electronic newsletter. It came out every week with updates on business trends, information about set-backs, even requests for input on upcoming decisions. We wanted employees to realize we wanted their thoughts, whether they agreed or disagreed.

"But we still had a lot to learn about communication."

"Like what?" asked one of the students.

"Well," Tom said, "we finally learned that communication is not just talk.

It's got to be action, too."

Tom went to the white board to summarize the third *Break-Point*:

BreakPoint #3: Communicating on Purpose

- Learn your communication style.

- Learn how to improve one-on-one communications.

- Use communications to improve the effectiveness of your leadership team.

- Learn how to communicate to large groups, inside and outside of your organization.

The MTG Story

*This is not an ownership decision,
it's a leadership decision.*

Don hadn't been on board more than six or seven months, Tom realized, and already MTG was running more efficiently. Don had been right about the value of process—the technicians had balked initially at the new deadlines for submitting paperwork, but billing was going much more smoothly and we were collecting money in a much more timely fashion. Susan was markedly less edgy, now that she could count on Tom to enforce the paperwork deadlines.

Renee still whined to Bob, but seemed to realize his clout had diminished, once Tom, as CEO, clearly became the ultimate authority on any decision. In fact, it was Bob who Tom found most irritating. Bob had mightily resisted Tom being named CEO. When Don followed up with the suggestion that MTG hire a sales executive to replace Tom, Bob had what, for him, amounted to a stroke.

"Hire another executive?" he exploded in their weekly management meeting. "That's another $75K against the budget! Why can't Tom continue selling and designate a day or two a week, or two or three hours a day, to handle the CEO duties?"

Don was calm but adamant. "Running the company is a fulltime job," he said. Managing the sales department is also a fulltime job. One guy can't do two fulltime jobs effectively."

This is just taking money off the top, when we're already tight," Bob responded.

"There's an old saying, "Penny-wise and pound foolish," Don said. "That means you can cut corners to save cash, but you'll lose more money in the end than if you make a responsible investment in getting the job done right. I'll guarantee you that hiring a sales manager will more than pay off in increased sales."

"I think he's right, Bob," said Tom. "We haven't been hitting our numbers as far as new clients go, because we've been so busy servicing the ones we have."

"I'm not ready to rush into this," Bob insisted.

"We're not rushing and we are going ahead," Tom responded. "We've discussed this as long as we're going to. I've listened to everyone and I'm making the decision—we're going to hire a sales manager."

And please, Bob, don't tell me again that you're a partner and can veto this decision. This is not an ownership decision, it's a leadership decision."

"We really do need to build sales," Tom was telling Rick Schwartz and Paul Green, during another golf outing. "I thought I was good—I know I have good contacts—but sales are stalled."

"Being a good salesman isn't the same as knowing how to build a sales engine—and that's what you want," said Paul. "You want someone to create a sales machine."

Rick nodded. "You've got to keep building the client list. Not only for the cash flow. It keeps everyone fresh and on their toes. Besides, Don's right—you can't do both jobs."

Paul replaced a club in his bag, then hoisted it on his shoulder. The trio didn't believe in carts; walking the fairways was part of the pleasure.

"Hey, I've got a great prospect for you," Paul said. "Melanie Stephens ..."

"Yeah, right!" Rick said. "I heard she's sick of all the travel at PRC—I think she's on the road eight weeks out of ten ..."

"Her kids are at that age when you've got to be home more than that," Paul added. "Even more important, Melanie is pure gold when it comes to creating a team. You oughta talk to her, feel her out."

"I'll do that," said Tom. "In fact, if either one of you sees her, test the waters for me. She sounds like someone we should consider bringing on board. Of course, Bob will have another fit—I'll bet Melanie is expensive if she's as good as you say," he added.

"She's every bit as good," said Rick. "And you know, you have to do something about Bob ..."

"That's right," Paul said, before Tom could respond.

"We're sick of hearing about Bob, aren't we Rick? He's a nice guy, smart in his field. But I don't think he's ever been in sync with your plans. You two have always been a strange couple."

Rick laughed and Tom nodded glumly as he lined up his putt. "Easier said than done. Bob's a partner—as he reminds me constantly—and there's no way to bring him in line. Believe me, I've tried."

***Why is this a big deal? Partners have conflicts.
They work them out.***

85

The following Tuesday, Don called a special partners'
meeting. Oddly, he summoned them to his office, not the
conference room, their usual meeting place. Seated behind
his desk, he emanated more authority than usual. Tom noticed
he was wearing a tie, another formality Don rarely observed.
His style was all about comfort and consensus—and he was
meticulously aware of his position as an administrator, not a
partner. Something was up.

"Gentlemen," he said, "I have an issue of some importance
I want to raise. It's something I believe will affect MTG's success
and it's something the three of you will have to decide. And
I'm sure the deliberations won't be easy."

Now all three partners knew something definitely was up.

"What is it?" asked Tom.

"To be blunt," Don responded. "I don't think your partnership is working effectively for MTG."

Jose shifted uneasily. Bob, characteristically, folded his
arms across his chest. Tom felt a little rush of adrenalin and
recognition. He hadn't discussed his golf conversation with
anyone except Amanda, so Don's comments came as a surprise.
But he knew Don was right. The partnership—specifically,
his relationship with Bob—wasn't working.

"It doesn't seem to me, as I've said before, that you three
are on the same page about where you are taking this company," said Don. "You have fairly deep disagreements about
growth strategy and your own investments of time, money
and commitment."

"Care to elaborate?" asked Bob. Jose remained quiet, his
usual tactic when disagreements developed. He didn't like

taking a strong position but, when push came to shove, he generally aligned himself with Tom.

"No, I really don't want to elaborate right at this moment," said Don. "I'm bringing this up so the three of you can think on it, talk about it and decide how—or if—you want to proceed.

"I'll be glad to talk with you individually about my observations, but I wanted to bring up the subject to all three of you at once so you know where I'm coming from.

"Each of you has obvious strengths and skills. All three of you are capable business leaders in your own way. The primary difference is in your willingness to take risks. This is all complicated by the differences in the equity each of you has in the company.

"It seems to me these things need to be resolved sooner, rather than later," he added.

"Resolution is going to be better not only for MTG, but for the three of you, too."

Bob spoke up again. "Why is this a big deal? Partners have conflicts. They work them out."

Don nodded.

"Yes, partners do sometimes find themselves at odds. Issue-by-issue, it's not a big deal. But when the same issues or problems keep coming up—and the root disagreement is never resolved—there's a constant friction in the organization.

"I'm no mechanical genius, but I do know this. Friction creates drag. It pulls your vehicle off course, slows it down. That's what it's doing here—wearing down the tires, putting extra strain on the engine. It's up to you three to eliminate the friction, one way or another."

— The Classroom —

BREAKPOINT #4
Partnership Pain

… hell, we didn't give it any thought!

"Well," Tom said to the class, "it was an uncomfortable moment. But Don was right. We all knew it. The partnership wasn't working because Bob and I were in conflict.

"I said it earlier. Jose and I didn't give much thought to what we were doing when we gave Bob equity—hell, we didn't give it any thought!"

Ten years of picking up dog poop can be a long, long time!

He paused for a moment.

"How many of you have a dog?" he asked. Several raised their hands.

"How many of you have dogs that want to travel?" The hands remained raised.

"How many of you with dogs think you might want to live in another country, spend nine months on a ship or engage in some other adventure?" Somewhat confused, nonetheless, a few raised their hands.

"How many of you thought, when you were getting your dog—saving it from the humane shelter, succumbing to its puppy-like charms or considering its value as a date magnet— thought to yourself,

Hey, a dog is a 10-to-15 year commitment. I'm going to have to feed it, walk it—and pick up its poop—until I'm, like, 40 years old. If I want to leave town, even for a day or two, I'm going to have to take the dog or find a place for it to stay.

No one raised a hand.

"Well," said Tom, "that's a lot of what it's like to give equity without thinking about the consequences. The dog may be cute, loyal as hell, warm on a lonely night and effective at attracting dates. But believe me, ten years of picking up dog poop can be a long, long time!"

The MTG Story

Are you staying because you want to—
or to prove you can?

It didn't take more than a few stilted conversations for the partners to realize they couldn't address—let alone resolve—their issues without help. Jo Murphy was due for a site visit; talking with her would at least be a place to begin. Tom asked Don to call Jo and bring her up to speed on his concerns.

She met first with Jose and asked the question she would ask all three partners: "What did you want out of the company when you started?"

"At first, I wanted to make money and be my own boss," Jose said. "I knew it meant a lot of hours and a lot of work, but that didn't bother me.

"I couldn't care less, really, about the business end. That's always been Tom's baby and he can have it, he's great at it.

"What turns me on is building something new. I'm my father's boy—I love to tinker. This business intelligence project I've been working on, we're way ahead on that. It's going to be big and we're going to make a ton of money, too. That's what jazzes me, building that thing."

"So what about the tensions between Tom and Bob?" Jo asked.

"I don't like to take sides," he told her. "Truthfully, Tom is usually right on the business decisions. If I can, I stay out of it. I feel bad for Bob, though. I guess he pictured himself as Tom's equal.

"I'll tell you one thing, though—I'm not having near as much fun at work as I used to. My concentration is way down and so is my satisfaction. Every time I know some big decision is coming up that's going to involve Tom and Bob having an argument, I get stomach problems.

"My wife knows how things are at work by how much time I spend in the bathroom."

We're worlds apart on what's best for the company.

Later that afternoon, Jo talked with Tom.

"What did I want from the company?" Tom said, repeating Jo's question. "At first, I didn't really know. I hadn't thought about it. I guess I saw us making a bundle of money. About the time I met Don, though, I figured out that I want to take MTG to the next level, whatever that is. We're good, but we're getting better. I want to see how far we can go."

"So what about the problems with Bob—what's happening with that?" Jo asked.

"What's happening? It's just not going away. We're talking more about the issues, but we're not getting anywhere. We just aren't on the same page. I want to invest in the company. Bob wants to pinch pennies. I say let's take a risk, he says we already take too many risks," Tom said.

"We're worlds apart on what's best for the company."

Jo purposefully met with Bob at the end of the day. She knew from past conversations that he wasn't happy. He didn't give her a chance to ease into the conversation.

"I may have made a mistake by getting into this partnership," he told her as soon as they sat down to dinner. "I got into this thinking it was my ticket to real financial stability—I've got kids, one who just graduated from college, one's in college and the third is a year away. I can't refinance the house again for tuition.

"I thought it would be great to work without a boss," he continues. "That's a joke—Tom is the boss. And he gets to tell me how I spend my money. He's always wanting to pour more money into 'growing the company' and I want to take some out to enjoy my life now! I don't want to grow the damn company. All those things I wanted aren't happening.

"It seems the more money we make, the more money we spend. Tom sees it as me pinching pennies, but when do we get to enjoy the fruits of our labor?" He looked at Jo. "Don't hug me!" he warned her.

She laughed—she had, indeed, been about to get up and give him a hug. Bob smiled, too. "No hugs, I'm beyond hugs," he said. "A hug won't fix it."

"What will fix it?" Jo asked. "Obviously you're not getting what you want and I'm guessing that Tom isn't, either."

"I don't know," Bob said. "I just don't want Tom to take me over the edge of financial ruin."

"Have you thought about whether you want to stay in the partnership? Have you considered taking another role in the company, where you feel like you have more *control*..."

"Control? I don't have any control!" he said.

"Don't you have control over how long you're willing to be miserable?" she asked. "Are you staying because you want to—or to prove you can?"

— *The Classroom* —

Partnership Pain

… partners must have a pre-nup!

"The upshot was that Jose and I bought out Bob's share. It took a while, it got complicated, but it was the right thing for all three of us.

"We were at different stages in what we wanted from life, specifically our work lives. It was causing more and more problems—from who should be CEO to how much money we should re-invest rather than distribute. I said it before—we didn't ask the right questions at the start."

He went to the whiteboard, marker in hand. "So, what are some questions you should ask the potential partner and yourself before offering equity?"

A young man raised his hand: "Ask if everyone understands that a partnership is like a marriage, except without the sex."

Laughter broke out.

"Oh, that is so true, in so many ways," Tom said. "I can't even begin to get into the nuances, but a business partnership can be every bit as fraught with difficulty as a marriage. To take the analogy even further—partners must have a pre-nup!"

He looked thoughtful.

"Jose and I—and even Bob—were like teenagers considering marriage. We had no idea what we were getting into. Not to beat this analogy to death, but we would have been better as friends with benefits."

"How so?" asked a student.

"What I know now," Tom responded, "is that most people who ask for equity really just want a share in the profit and a piece of the proceeds if the business is ever sold. Equity—as in partnership—includes those two things, but it does have downsides.

"If the business needs a loan, the bank will require a personal guarantee from the partners. If the business needs $100,000 and you own 20 percent, you're in for $20,000.

"We didn't fully understand that fact. If we had, and if we had explained it to Bob, he would have never wanted to be a partner."

"What could you have done differently?" someone asked.

"We could have given Bob 'phantom' stock," Tom answered. "What Bob really wanted was a chunk of cash if we sold the company. There are a lot of ways to write an agreement that grants financial benefits without incurring risks—and without giving that employee the power of ownership. Just because you own 10 to 20 percent of a company's stock doesn't mean you have a say in day-to-day operations. Unless, of course, you're Warren Buffet.

"This gets back to the point I made earlier: Don't be afraid to ask for expert advice. We didn't do that when we started. We downloaded some forms, filled them out and had them notarized. If we had asked a business lawyer or a consultant like Don for help, we could have avoided a whole lot of hassle.

We didn't ask the right questions at the start.

"So, one of the first questions to ask yourself, even if you aren't considering bringing a partner on board immediately, is, 'How will we value the company and the new partner's contribution?' What would make it worthwhile to give equity without a cash investment?"

He returned to the whiteboard.

"Alright. For whatever reasons, you've decided you want to bring on a partner. You've vetted for skill sets and reputation and you think personalities will mesh. What questions do you ask?"

- How do you see us exiting this business? Are you comfortable including a buy/sell agreement as part of the partnership agreement?

- What do you need to earn annually? What would you like to take home? Are there events that will affect those figures—college tuitions, weddings?

- Do we all understand that equity means not only sharing profits but also reinvestment expenses?

- What is your credit history? ("Banks require good credit history to advance credit," said Tom.)

- How liquid are your assets? ("Just like a marriage," he said. "You've got to be upfront about finances.")

- Partners are personally liable for corporate debts. Do you have personal financial assets—and can you afford to lose them—to fulfill that obligation?

- Will you pony up for help if the company needs consultants with expertise? Will you put your ego aside, your wallet on the table?

- What hours do you expect to work? Are you at a stage in life where you want to be a nine-to-fiver? Will you sacrifice outside activities while building the company? Do you have travel constraints or other personal obligations that could keep you from meeting expectations of the partnership?

"I've skipped a couple important points I want to stress," Tom said.

"First of all, it's important to ask what keeps a potential partner up at night—what worries them, stresses them out? What scares them the most about the business they're in, what excites them most?

"Another thing—you've heard this before—how do they communicate? Are they willing to reveal themselves to a partner? Can they accept constructive criticism?

"And one final thing. Don't underestimate this one: Is the person's spouse in agreement with the level of commitment— the financial, time and emotional commitment—to the company? If not, that will cause a problem, either in the partnership or the family relationship."

"See," said the student who'd spoken up earlier. "It always comes back to marriage."

Tom went to the white board:

BreakPoint #4: Partnership Pain

• "Date" long enough to know the "marriage" will last.

• Talk money, skills and values and interests.

• Sign a "pre-nup" to cover the end of the partnership.

"Guys, see you next week," he said, putting down the marker.

The MTG Story

Recruit, recruit and then recruit some more.

Melanie Stephens was not an easy hire for MTG. She had glowing recommendations from Rick Schwartz and Paul Green, but Tom was determined not to make a hiring mistake this time. Before bringing Melanie in for an interview, he worked with Don and Jo on his evaluation criteria. He'd done a little research on the qualities of a great sales manager—as opposed to a great sales person—and wanted to see whether Melanie fit the criteria.

"What makes a great sales manager?" he asked in their first meeting, after the opening formalities and chitchat. Melanie didn't hesitate for even a microsecond.

"First thing: Recruit, recruit and then recruit some more," she responded. "Make sure your next great sales guy is in the bullpen.

"Second thing: Understand your metrics for success. How long from sales pitch to sales close? How do you manage your funnel? What percent of gross profit is spent on sales? What percentage of leads convert to sales? Do you know what good—much less great—looks like for these metrics against your competitors?

"If you can't measure it, you can't manage it," she said.

"Third thing: Own your sales process. Know how it works, why it works and be able to teach it to your people. And—this is crucial—insist they use it, even if they think theirs is better.

"Last thing: Own your sales number. It's yours. Deliver it come hell or high water."

Tom had heard—and would learn first-hand—that Melanie was a pro at all four.

"I've got a question for you," she continued, without waiting for his next question. "What's keeping MTG from growing as fast as Rick and Paul think it can? They tell me it's got great potential."

Tom felt an instant connection. "She's as up-front as I am," he thought. She was clearly vetting MTG to see if the company met her standards.

"I don't know," he answered. "We've got good people, good service. I think we're responsive. But our sales just aren't as predictable as they should be."

"Well," she said, with the slight accent that revealed Southern roots, "that's definitely something I can fix."

What's keeping MTG from growing as fast as Rick and Paul think it can?

Tom was biting nails until she accepted the position as VP of Sales and Marketing—and was grateful when she did.

— *The Classroom* —

BREAKPOINT #5

Revving the Engine

*If the average candidate doesn't reach out to me,
they don't get the next interview.*

"Okay, let's get going, guys," Tom said, hurrying his students to their seats. "I've talked to you about MTG's sales machine. Now here she is, the driver and pit boss, Melanie Stephens.

"Remember, Don said we needed a sales manager. In my naiveté, I thought that meant another sales person who could handle the administrative stuff, too. When I met Melanie, I realized I didn't have a clue. A sales manager is a different animal."

He turned to the "pit boss," MTG's forty-something sales manager. Melanie had an edgy glamour, with a tailored designer suit, high heels and enough gold jewelry to signal success without going over the line to excess. The glint in her eyes suggested she was capable of using the rock on her left ring finger as a weapon, when necessary, to get what she wanted.

"Melanie, would you describe your training for the class?

"Sure," she replied. "I graduated from this fine university with a business degree and went directly to Xerox. They put me in sales training right away. I've got a talent for teaching the sales process ..."

"And managing it," Tom interjected.

"Yes," she agreed. "I moved right up Xerox's ladder for six years, then jumped to PRC as a regional manager. It wasn't too long before I snagged a national position, handling sales for the eastern half of the country. I'm happy to say we exceeded our targets every year."

Tom stepped in. "A lot of people have good credentials. What makes you so much more effective than the rest?" Melanie took over the podium, thanked Tom, and turned to the students.

"As Tom told you, I believe a great sales manager is constantly recruiting good people, knows how to measure how good they are, has a process for teaching them to be better and is absolutely committed to consistently hitting her sales goals.

"That all starts with hiring. It's like picking a jury in a murder case—if you haven't picked the right people before the first witness takes the stand, it almost doesn't matter how good your evidence is, you aren't going to get a conviction. That's why I'm so dedicated to my hiring process." She handed Tom a stack of papers to pass around.

"The process has five steps," she continued. "I'm giving you a synopsis so you can follow along.

"After I've identified a candidate—and, as Tom said, I'm always looking for good recruits—I like to bring them in and let them know what a great place MTG is to work."

She scrawled on the white board:

Step One: Sell the Company to the Candidate

"This isn't a job interview," she said. "In fact, there might not even be a job. I could just be taking an interesting prospect to lunch. I want them to visualize themselves achieving their goals at my company. If I can get all the fish in the lake jumping into the boat, then I can decide which ones are big enough to keep.

"Here's the key point. I let them know it's their responsibility to get back in touch and schedule our next meeting. Doesn't matter how eager I am to get that person—I want to know if he or she is going to follow through on that simple commitment. If they do, they move to the next step."

A student raised her hand. "So you never pursue a candidate, even if they are the best?"

"There are some exceptions," Melanie said. "But only for absolute top recruits. Remember, I've sold them on MTG. If the average candidate doesn't reach out to me, they don't get the next interview."

Step Two: A Behavioral Interview

"I've got a list of twenty job-related questions—I'll hand out a copy later. These questions require a real-life example of how the candidate reacted to a past experience. Their answers tell me how they'll behave in specific types of sales transactions. I tell them we'll review their answers and my reactions at the end of the interview."

The student raised her hand again. "Your candidates have to answer all twenty questions?" she asked.

"Good question," Melanie responded. "No, I pick six or eight questions, based on the candidate and what I see as their target market. There are two or three questions I always ask.

"For example, I always ask 'How have you responded to a prospect who says your price is too high?' I generally get one of two answers.

"The first is what I call the value track—'I must not have told you how wonderful our product is.' The second I call the horse-trader—'If we lower the price today, will we have a deal?' Most candidates pick one track or the other, but neither is a great answer.

"The best is to answer the question with a question. You get more information about which road your customer is going down, the value track or the horse-trading track.

"Mainly, whatever answer I get from the candidate, it's an opportunity for feedback in the second part of the interview." She took a sip of water before continuing.

"I break it down into things I like and areas where I think they can improve. And I always give two to three times more positive feedback than negative. What I'm looking for is how they take my feedback.

"If the candidate responds to every criticism by defending his answers, it indicates to me that person is not going to be very coachable. If she takes the feedback and thanks me for it—if I think she gets the point—I know she's coach-able and willing to learn from me.

"I can't help people that aren't coach-able or who don't want to do things my way," she said. "Very rarely, if I come across someone who really knows what he's doing and isn't coach-able, I'll hire him anyway, and let him take the reins in getting business. Very rarely."

Step Three: The Ride-Along

She capped her marker and turned back to the class. "I hook up the candidate with a salesperson for a day. I tell that employee to be completely honest in answering questions about the company—the good and the bad. Typically, by that point, we're interested in hiring. But I want the candidate to be sure it's going to be a good fit."

Will he or she ask for the job?

Step Four: Writing a Business Plan

"This step is devilishly two-edged," she said.

"I ask for a one-page business plan on how the person would develop their territory for us. It has to include a sales goal. If they come back with a low goal, we generally don't hire them—we want people who are really hungry and ambitious.

"Now here's the devilish part. Usually a good candidate is going to come up with a stretch goal—not necessarily easy to meet. If we hire them, it gives us a starting point for structuring their compensation against the goal they set themselves. It's also helped us establish a solid baseline, over the years, for new sales reps.

"If the plan looks good, we take the last step."

Step Five: The Final Interview

"By this time, I'm ready to hire. I've used the candidate's business and marketing plan to create a compensation illustration that shows how much money he or she will make. And I've incorporated their marketing plan into our ramp process to show how they can meet their goals.

"But before I get to that, I'm looking for just one thing from the candidate: Will he or she ask for the job? If a candidate isn't willing to ask for the job, he's probably not going to ask for the order to close a sale. If you can't or won't ask, we don't close. It's that simple."

The MTG Story

Let's make sure our seat belts are buckled.

"Come on in," Melanie said when Tom and Jose appeared at her office door.

She had spent her first two months at MTG evaluating the three-person sales team, as well as its sales and marketing practices. They had set aside a good part of this afternoon for her conclusions and recommendations. Tom and Jose settled into club chairs while Melanie took her seat behind the desk.

"How bad is it?" Tom asked, half joking, half not.

"Not as bad as I feared," Melanie responded in the same light vein. "No, really, there are some issues—but we have a lot of strengths, too. We've definitely got a foundation to work with.

"Before we talk about the sales team and sales structure, we need to address some support issues."

"Such as?" asked Tom.

"Such as—there isn't a support structure, or the one that's there is barely functional," she said. "The sales team can't concentrate on sales.

"It's like you're running a dairy. Besides sales, y'all are sending these poor folks out to milk the cows, come back and make the cheese—then shovel the manure out and clean the barns, too."

Her sly smile indicated she was pouring on her normally slight Georgia accent for effect.

"You've got Susan handling client demands for all three

sales people plus you, Tom. She's good but she doesn't have a sales background. Then Rachel, in operations—who, FYI, scares the hell out of sales with her rules and rants—is trying to control them when everyone knows you can't corral a great salesperson. Fulfillment is getting spotty and the clients are restless."

Tom and Jose both nodded.

"So Point 1: We need one support person in the office for every two to three sales people. I've lined up training for Susan, and I'm cherry-picking my favorite administrative aide from PRC—she starts in three weeks.

"Point 2: Generating demand for product—we don't have a system, other than what sales people do individually. Personal networking only takes us so far. We need to scale up demand and then turn sales loose on 'em.

"That'll give us sales predictability, so we know what we have to manage," she said. "I'm amazed you've been able to get this far, working with such inconsistent sales.

"Here's the thing. A good sales person develops momentum, working with a pile of leads. If he has to stop selling every few weeks to drum up more leads, he has to rebuild the momentum when he gets out to make sales again.

"That's inefficient. We need a couple of systems to generate leads for outside sales.

"We've thought about starting telemarketing...,"

Jose started. He then caught himself. Melanie had the same tendency as Tom to take shortcuts through her thoughts. Jose wasn't yet as in tune with her shortcuts as he was with Tom's.

"I'm setting up a department," Melanie said, answering

Jose's silent question. "We'll get four or five kids right out of college, put a couple of 'em on phones to start, dialing for warm leads.

"But we've got to get into social media—we're an IT company, right? I haven't decided which platforms, Facebook, LinkedIn, Twitter, whatever. I'm going to let the brightest kids develop a blog, email, maybe even videos. These kids come out of school writing apps for their iPads. We're going to take advantage of that."

"This is something we should do right away?" Jose asked.

"Absolutely," Melanie responded. "Here's why. In my experience, most good companies have either a great sales team or great customer service. Only the best have both.

"We're already way ahead on service. That's part of what made me want this job—you have a real commitment to your customers. What we don't have—yet—is a great sales team. Creating a lead-generating process is a big step toward that goal.

"At the same time, we'll be getting a farm system for new sales reps. We don't have enough great sales people worth hiring in our market. We'll grow our own on the lead generating team. The best will end up in outside sales. With any luck, the bad ones will quit before we have to fire them." Tom had never seen anything but unfailing charm from Melanie in a sales situation. But when it came to management meetings, she cut right to the point.

"To my third point," she said. "MTG has the best internal communications systems I've seen—my God, everyone's up on what everyone else is doing. And I mean that in a good way.

"But there's no external communication. We've got to let people know we're here, go to some industry conferences, talk ourselves up, get a marketing program in place. We'll dovetail it with our social media efforts. I'll work up the details while we're getting sales support and demand generation in place."

She ticked an item off the printout in front of her.

"Now, one more thing," she said.

"Jose, your product is great, really great. We're going to sell the hell out of it. It's going to be a big fat revenue stream for us and, as soon as you get it past beta, we'll start a dedicated sales operation."

Jose, who'd been a little bored by the sales talk but mesmerized by Melanie's staccato delivery, now looked stunned.

"You have no idea how different it is to have a proprietary product," she said. "It will change MTG, if we handle it correctly, which we will. But that's a whole other meeting. We don't need to tangle with it now."

Jose was gathering his thoughts to say something but Melanie had put her printout aside. She moved three manila folders to the center of her desk. Tom took it as a signal to move for a break.

"Back in fifteen," he said, BlackBerry in hand. Both Jose and Melanie began tapping their keyboards as well.

But we've got to get into social media—we're an IT company, right?

When the meeting resumed, all three executives were eager to get to the heart of the matter—Melanie's evaluation of MTG's three-person sales team.

"Well, that's the chassis, guys," she said, referring to their decisions on the sales support structure. "Let's get to the engine."

"Basically, I informally ran Jason, Steven and Barbara through my recruitment process, just to see where we are. I did a ride-along with each of them and ran their numbers through my metrics for each of the last nine months."

"And?" asked Tom.

"Two-thirds good, one-third shaky—very shaky," said Melanie. "Barbara is close to my ideal and Jason, even though he's more independent than I usually like, is a good producer. Steve, I think, is going to be a no-go. But let me start with the good news.

"Jason's a hunter. He hits his number every month, he's got a good local network and brings in a lot of new business. On the downside, his customer satisfaction is iffy. We can take care of that when we revamp sales support.

"As I said, he does like to go his own way—which is not my preference. My process is tried and true. I'd like everyone using it. But Jason's system is working up to my standards, so I'm going to let it be. Let's say he's 'grandfathered in.'

"Barbara is a natural. She strategizes and all her strategies are good. She works pretty much along the same lines I do. I think a few tweaks will make her even better. She meets with reps from non-competing companies to share sales leads. That's something I'm going to incorporate into our program."

"Her communication style is excellent, she's competitive but collaborative. I plan to bring her along so she'll be ready to roll out Jose's product when it launches."

"Now the bad news," said Jose.

"Steve is a problem," Melanie said. "He thinks he's a heavy-hitter. I disagree. His month-to-month figures are Mt. Everest one month, Death Valley the next. He can't focus on more than one project at a time. Clients are like potato chips—you can't have just one. I need my people to multi-task."

Tom felt a twinge of recognition. Steve was always on the verge of closing a big deal that was just out of reach. Yet he was so personable, Tom thought he would eventually pull it off.

"Steve's been building contacts at some big firms. It takes time to get up the ladder to the top guys."

Melanie closed Steve's file. "Let me tell you—Barb's got some home runs in the works and so does Jason. Meanwhile, they keep the base hits coming and make their numbers every month.

"I'll work with Steve for another month or two. But I don't think he's coach-able. He's convinced he knows it all. He tells me he has twenty years of sales experience. What he has is one year of sales experience, which he's repeated for twenty years.

"There might be some other job here for him, but I can't imagine what it would be. I've seen lots of 'Steves' along the way. In the end, they don't produce at the level I demand and they have a hard time stepping into a less glamorous role from sales."

"In the meantime," she said, putting away all three files, "I've got my eye on some great future prospects."

Everything Melanie said rang true, including the trouble spots. And her take on Jose's project was a bonus.

"Ten years in business and I had no idea what a babe-in-the-woods I really was," Tom thought. To Melanie, he said, "You are incredible!"

"I know," she agreed, as Tom and Jose got up to leave.

"She scares me," Jose said, as soon as they were out of earshot.

"Yeah, me too—but in a good way," Tom said. "Every time I talk to her, I learn something new about sales."

"Not sales—about building a sales machine," said Jose, repeating one of Melanie's favorite phrases.

"I think we're going to have to straighten up and become a real business," Tom replied.

"This lady is going to take us to a whole new level."

"I know," Jose said, pulling out his car keys and heading for the lobby door. "Let's make sure our seat belts are buckled."

— *The Classroom* —

BREAKPOINT #5
Revving the Engine

if you can't measure it, you can't manage it.

From his seat among his grad students, Tom pointed out that Melanie's hiring process could have taken a month or longer.

"But it paid off," he said. "More than half her hires were successful and stayed on-board for years. Before Melanie arrived, we probably cycled through more than two-dozen sales people. And there were only three people on the team when she got there.

"What amazed me was her ability to assess a recruit's success within a few months based upon activity and approach—when I was managing sales, it took me between twelve and sixteen months to know if someone would be successful by looking at the "sum total" line. That's very expensive. I kept non-producers much longer than I should have. That's not to say that I didn't see any gaps in their sales approach. But I couldn't identify those problems, so, of course, I couldn't help fix them—it required an experience and skill, I didn't have."

"Melanie, how are you able to make your assessments so quickly?"

"Two words—metrics and process," she answered.

"But before I talk about those, I want to point out that when I got to MTG, Tom was managing three sales people. Now I didn't say he was managing a sales department—because he wasn't. He was managing each of those people individually, basically just looking at their volume and letting them figure out the best way to sell.

"That might be fine for a department of three people," she continued. "But the department isn't going to grow, because it's not going to be successful over time. If it does happen to grow, it can't get very big because it's not efficient to manage more than three people individually."

A student raised his hand, but Melanie raised her own hands.

"I know what you're going to say," she said. "I'm not saying I don't give individual attention to people—but I give it to them within the standards I've created. And that brings me back to metrics and process.

"I've always said, 'If you can't measure it, you can't manage it.' Metrics are the standards for measuring a sales person's progress. 'Almost' doesn't matter what they are, so long as they're consistent.

"Nothing's perfect, but I can use metrics, not only to measure someone's success early on, but also to improve their progress. So we set up a funnel process at MTG for all our new hires, tracking them on a number of metrics.

"We look at how many calls they made on a weekly basis. How many of those calls turned into appointments. How many appointments turned into proposals and finally, how many of those turned into sales. I can look at those results and see where a person is struggling—maybe they don't make enough appointments or they can't close. Now I know where they need help."

"The key for me is knowing what the metrics should be telling me, if someone is going to prove their worth. For MTG, that was $500,000 annually in gross profit. Once they hit that threshold, we didn't need to track them so closely."

Tom had another question: "How could you help them get over a hump, since everybody has their own style? What works for one might not work for another."

"You're right. I'm not looking for cookie-cutter personalities—there are all kinds of good sales people. It's like food. Some people like fast, hot, greasy, salty and sweet. Others want subtle, sophisticated food.

"I can work with a person's individual strengths or style," she said, smiling broadly. "But when they work for me, their style has to fit my process. I've worked it, I know it works and I want everyone on my sales team using it. With very few exceptions, if they don't like my process—well, then, they can go manage their own damn departments!"

We had done enough right with the company that we got beyond the point of hiring good— we could hire the best.

Tom stepped up with his final question.

"Melanie, you were obviously very successful on a much larger scale than MTG—PRC's a national company. It has a thousand employees and you were in charge of sales for half the country. MTG had maybe twenty-five employees when you started—just three in sales. We were the little local guys. How did we persuade you to come on board?"

"You didn't persuade me," Melanie said. "What you did was present me with an opportunity. It was inevitable that I would leave PRC.

"I had a lot of responsibilities, a lot of perks, a lot of power. I was on the road three weeks out of four—which is great, at first. Then you get tired of the hotel rooms, even the nice ones, and the restaurant meals, even the good ones. You really get tired of the airports.

"I've got kids—and I don't care how great technology is, Skyping the bedtime story does not work.

"I discussed all this with my VP. They didn't want to lose me—but we agreed there wasn't anything on the horizon for me at PRC.

"Along comes Tom. He's got a great little company, but doesn't know how to make it bigger," she continued. "And there's Jose. He's building a product so good, it's a separate revenue stream. Which Tom and Jose kind of realize, but they're not sure what to do about it.

"Not only that, they're known for their customer service. They go above and beyond to come up with the right solution. That's half the distance to great right there.

"Their sales division is struggling—and I like that! What's the point of going in and managing something that's working?

"So if I take over their sales operation, I'm not only able to kiss my kids goodnight, I get to build something. I can create a dynamite sales team from the ground up and add significant value—something they honestly could not do without me. There's a lot of satisfaction in that."

Tom took over.

"This all gets back to hiring good people," he said. "We had done enough "right" with the company that we got beyond the point of hiring good—we could hire the best."

Tom went to the white board to summarize the key components of the *BreakPoint*:

BreakPoint #5: Revving the Engine

- "Best sales person" does not equal "best sales manager."

- Develop a recruiting/hiring process.

- Know the numbers you need to succeed.

- Use every available sales avenue.

The MTG Story

I think we're about at our limit.

Tom arrived home around 7 p.m., kicked off his loafers and let his kids rough him up a little. Amanda brought a tray of drinks and snacks to the screened porch, before sending the boys out to catch fireflies.

"Busy day?" Amanda asked. Tom put his feet up on the wicker coffee table.

"Oh, man, busy isn't the half of it," he said. "I feel like I've traded in a Toyota for a Maserati. It's great but who knew driving a race car took so much energy!"

Melanie Stephens had turbo-charged MTG's sales team, giving the whole company a blast of high-octane energy. She implemented her training program, kicked sales lead generation up a notch and had her people hitting—and exceeding—their sales goals within the first year. Changes in the second year were more gradual, but steady.

Now, between the new sales people, their support teams, a small marketing department focused on Jose's product, as well as additional technical employees to meet increased demand, the company had grown to nearly 60 people. All good, Tom assured his wife.

"But I think we're about at our limit," he told her. "In a way, I feel like I did at the start—wondering whether I can keep all the balls in the air. Not to mention the Rachel problem."

"She and Melanie get into it again today?" Amanda asked.

"Again? It never really stops," Tom replied. "I'm golfing with Paul and Rick tomorrow, and I think I'm going to bring Rick in for a week. We've got to find some long-term solutions."

Rachel had been prickly and difficult even before Melanie's arrival. She never trusted anyone on the sales team, not even Tom. When he talked to her about it, she insisted they weren't reliable—even went so far as saying they lied.

"Are you kidding me?" Tom had said, the first time she made the accusation. "That just can't be!"

"It is," Rachel insisted. "At least three times a month, some client comes in and says he was told the system would do either "X, Y or Z," even though that's not what I heard.

"I go back to the reps to see if they said that—and they say 'no' or they can't remember. They 'can't remember' and I'm stuck with the unhappy client."

"Rachel, you're right—that can't happen. But they're not lying. They're pitching ten different products with twenty different features to two or three prospects a day.

"I do it myself—keep throwing things against the wall 'til I see a light bulb go off over the guy's head. Then I go in for the kill. I forget half of what I told 'em in the first place. In the meantime, they 'remember' that I promised them everything.

"I'll work it out with sales, get them to stick to the job packages better."

He wondered if MTG was barreling toward big success—or disaster.

And he had, as much as he could. But he couldn't change Rachel. She didn't cut anyone any slack—if the details weren't exactly the way she demanded, she couldn't do her job. Worse, she tended to hire other micro-managers. Her whole department felt chilly. Even customers complained. Tom figured those were the tradeoffs for making sure projects got done.

Then Melanie arrived and wanted to make some changes. Rachel wouldn't budge. She didn't care how many times Melanie demonstrated how things could be done more efficiently. She'd been there ten years. She wanted things done her way.

In the meantime, Melanie and her team were landing bigger projects. They had an RFP from an existing client that was penciling out to about $3.5 million. If they got it, the job would be MTG's biggest ever, but they'd have to make a big upfront investment.

On top of all that, Don pointed out they were outgrowing the accounting system and Melanie was pushing for investment in more sophisticated tools to manage sales.

Jose's project was moving along, leaving him little time to confer with Tom on the big financial decisions. Agendas for the monthly strategy meetings were meaty, to say the least.

Tom relied on his conversations with Amanda, weekly phone conferences with Jo, peer group meetings and frequent consultation with Rich Schwartz to keep everything on track. But, as he decompressed on the porch with his wife, he wondered if MTG was barreling toward big success—or disaster.

— The Classroom —

BREAKPOINT #6
Changing the Guard

Hire 'lite' but hire right.

Tom sent a two-pound box of See's Candy around the classroom as soon as his grad students were seated.

"No pinching the candies," he said. "We're going to watch a video, so I brought you a little treat."

He hit play and the YouTube logo appeared on the screen. "You guys are way too young to remember 'I Love Lucy,' but this is a classic," he said, as the Candy Factory episode from 1952 began. Lucy and Ethel, in uniforms and aprons, are wrapping chocolates from a conveyor belt. "Wrap the chocolates and put them back on the belt," they've been told. "If any unwrapped candy gets into the next room, you'll be fired!"

All goes well, for the first few candies. Then the girls fall behind—way behind. They snatch candies off the belt, wrap madly and pop chocolates in their mouths to keep them from passing into the boxing room. Hearing their boss approach, the two cram candies into their mouths, down their necklines and into their hats. The boss, seeing no unwrapped candies—nor Lucy and Ethel's bulging cheeks—congratulates them and yells to the belt operator: "Okay, speed it up!"

"That's the most famous episode ever of *I Love Lucy*," Tom tells the class as the three-minute clip ended. "And that's how I was starting to feel at MTG, a year or two after we hired Melanie."

"How so? I thought she was great?" someone asked, as the box of candy went around the room again.

"She was great," Tom replied. "But it was like putting a Maserati engine in a used Ford. The rest of us couldn't keep up. Melanie is a top-notch expert. She kind of threw the company out of balance. To steal a 'Don-ism,' it was like working your traps and delts without paying attention to your pecs."

"What'd you do?" asked another student.

"What do you think I should have done?" Tom parried.

"Gone to the gym and worked your pecs?"

"Ri-i-i-i-ght," said Tom. "Anyone else?"

"Beef up the other departments," offered someone else.

"By doing what?" Tom replied.

"Bringing in more experts?" said a student sitting toward the back.

"Bingo!" said Tom.

"Rick convinced me it was time to get serious. He and I had done some pretty intense work, coming up with guiding principles for making decisions," Tom said. "We'd made decisions all the time, of course. The meeting rhythm we developed really helped us make 'em more efficient. But they were pretty ad hoc. Rick said we needed criteria that could be repeated, so everyone in the company was working off the same principles.

"That was working for us, but Rick persuaded me we needed another executive and we should hire a recruiter to find the right person."

Tom grinned. "It was going to cost us $30,000. Can you imagine what Bob would have said?"

After the laughter died down, Tom continued.

"This wasn't just a flyer we took," he said. "I really did—kind of—think of what Bob would have said. We'd been talking about additional management costs in my peer group, and we had a speaker who really convinced me that the flatter your management structure, the more profitable the company. In a company the size of MTG, management shouldn't cost more than five or six percent of gross margin.

"Yeah, yeah, I know," he said, noting a few raised eyebrows in the room. "It took us ten years but we'd gotten with the whole professional thing—I can sling benchmarks with the best of 'em.

"Anyway, it gets back to *BreakPoint #2*—hire the right people. I call it hire 'lite' but hire right. We hire as good as we can get.

"In this case, that $30K on recruiting was absolutely the best money I ever spent. We found Walter Jones in Atlanta. He was working for an IT integration firm but wanted to bring his family back to St. Louis to be near his parents. He's been a great VP of engineering—he couldn't be more different than Bob. Great experience, absolutely no drama."

"Did you have to do anything special to get him?" asked a student.

We vested them over five years, based on specific growth milestones.

"Good question—as a matter of fact, we did," Tom said. "He wanted equity ..." Several in the class groaned.

"I know, I know," Tom said, holding up his hands. "But we were a lot smarter this time around. We offered both Walter and Melanie a small piece of the business, since we'd finished buying out Bob. But we vested them over five years, based on specific growth milestones. Believe me, we had a very detailed agreement!"

The MTG Story

After more than a decade, Tom thought the growing pains should be over.

Tom's glass of champagne sat on his desk, untouched. Jose sat across from him, sneakered feet on the desk, texting his wife. Outside the glass wall of Tom's office, the last few staff members were draining their own glasses of champagne, congratulating the sales team and pulling on coats to go home. Melanie and Walter accepted final congratulations as Don gathered debris from the celebration. MTG had landed the $3.5 million contract, the project Melanie's staff had been pursuing for 18 months.

Walter had come along just in time to ensure Operations would be able to deliver what Sales promised. Even so, there were plenty of problems that would demand attention in the coming year. There were already odd little problems popping up that had never previously popped—accounting issues, a sexual harassment complaint, irritable employees gathering around the virtual water cooler, which they'd never done before.

After more than a decade, Tom thought the growing pains should be over. Apparently that wasn't true. Walter and Melanie had smoothed the road, but their own divisions kept them too busy to help out much with the business in general.

Tom thought about the time he'd changed a muffler on his first car, a Volkswagen Beetle. There'd been an unreachable bolt and another with a frozen nut. He and a high school buddy spent all day getting the damn muffler out and the new one in. A mechanic would have done it in an hour. Walter, he thought, was a mechanic—and thank God for that!

Rachel was not a mechanic. No, thought Tom as his thoughts jumped, she was more and more like a sticky valve. It was becoming increasingly evident that, compared to the high-octane performances of Walter and Melanie, Rachel was no longer up to the task of managing her department. The demand had grown exponentially and, despite continual training, her skills had not kept up with the growth.

Worse, thought Tom, it was becoming apparent that the company had also outgrown Don's skill sets. Both he and Rachel were struggling, not only to perform, but to keep their footing in the faster-paced atmosphere of the company. Don was handling a lot of the financials and some of the personnel responsibilities but he had said more than once that he wasn't familiar with the complexities of several issues. Don and Rachel—once among MTG's most experienced employees—were now learning on the job.

MTG could not afford that luxury.

When Jose hit the disconnect button on his phone, Tom took the opportunity to raise the topic. It wasn't the first time; they had tiptoed around the issue a few times in the past six weeks but Tom decided to plunge in completely, this time.

"What are we going to do about Don and Rachel?" he asked. Jose groaned.

"You sure know how to kill a good time, don't you?" he responded. "Can't a guy coast on his laurels for even an hour without being brought back to earth?"

"I know, but I've been sick about it for weeks. Don is

practically family. If it weren't for him, we'd still be working out of coffee shops. And Rachel's a pain, but she's been around from the start, too. I think her kid's in middle school and her mother just moved in. I feel like I'd be canning my sister-in-law. Don—that'd be like killing my dad."

"Yeah. The dark side of success," said Jose.

We need a CFO.

The next morning, Don sauntered into Tom's office 30 minutes before the weekly strategy meeting. "Got a minute?" he asked, taking the seat Jose had occupied the night before.

"Of course," Tom replied. "Don't tell me—it's your anniversary and you want my advice on where to take Marian."

"Uh, no," Don said. "I wanted to touch base on a few things that are breaking in accounting. And when I say 'breaking,' I mean that literally. And not in a good way, either."

"What?" asked Tom.

"We've got to upgrade the system, especially with this big deal going down. We'll need it even more when Jose's project hits full stride. I've done a little research but ..."

"Tom, I can't take responsibility for finding the right system ..."

Tom interrupted him, "We'll all be taking responsibility, you know that."

Don raised his hands in a reassuring gesture. "I know. Yeah, I know. But we've always been upfront. That's been me from the start and even more so after working with you. This thing, these accounting issues are beyond me, Tom."

129

"We'll bring in a consultant. Jeez, we're up to what—84 employees? And Melanie's deal is going to require its own little system. Not a problem—in fact, it's a good idea to get someone in to assess the situation and make recommendations. We'll put it on the agenda for today's meeting."

Don steepled his fingers under his chin and looked across the desk at Tom. He still didn't wear a tie, his slacks were Dockers and Tom wondered why he hadn't noticed before now that Don was wearing those crepe-soled shoes with square toes that Tom associated with men on the edge of retirement.

"What?" he asked Don.

"You know what," Don answered. "We need a CFO. For that matter, we need a pro in HR, too."

"We can't do that," said Tom. Something fluttered underneath his diaphragm. It wasn't a good flutter, either.

"If we did that, what would you and I do?"

Don looked at him again, letting a beat of silence pass.

"You two—you and Jose—were such kids," he said.

"Ambitious, eager, ready for take-off..."

Tom chuckled. "Yeah, weren't we? Thank God you came along."

It was getting close to their scheduled meeting. Melanie, Walter and Jose would be at the door in a minute or two. Something unspoken passed between the two men. Tom tried to ignore it but Don wouldn't let him.

"Think about it, Tom," Don said. "I'm thinking about it. I've been here, what, eight years? Nine? You guys have made it—and I gotta say, I know I helped. I feel great about that, I really do. I think I've got another company in me, though, before I head for Arizona...."

There were times, Tom thought, when it was just so much more comfortable not to face things head on. That's just how he felt now. Don was obviously talking about leaving MTG and, while Tom was relieved that Don's exit would be graceful, he was saddened by the prospect. Jose and Melanie's arrival at that moment was a welcome diversion.

BREAKPOINT #6

Changing the Guard

*Loyalty has to switch from the individual employees
to the organization itself.*

"Having Don leave MTG was one of the hardest things I was ever involved with in my years of doing business," Tom told his seminar students. "If it hadn't been for him, Jose and I would probably have been back working for a salary and paying off debts from MTG that would have lasted a lifetime. Don was literally our savior.

"But you know what?" he asked the class, uncharacteristically taking a seat in the circle of chairs. "It was just like Don to push us to push him to exit the company."

"A final lesson?" asked a usually quiet student to Tom's left.

"Exactly," said Tom. "And he showed us how to do it, too. I started looking around, keeping an eye out for opportunities for Don. Like he said, he was ready for a new challenge. With us, he'd moved beyond the really small company he'd been with before and he taught us a lot and learned a lot. But he knew—and I knew—we were suddenly beyond him. I would have kept him there forever if I had to, but he wasn't going to settle for that. Like he said, he had another company in him."

"What did he mean?" asked another student. "Did he tell you he wanted to leave?"

Tom considered the question. "You know, it's funny. We were all about open communication and transparency. But when it came to exiting, Don—and Rachel, too, for that matter—we weren't as upfront as we usually were. I mean, Don didn't let us sweep the issue under the rug, don't get me wrong. It was like knowing your grandmother isn't going to be around forever. We danced around a little, touched on the issue, backed off.

"I just felt an intense loyalty to Don, and to Rachel, too. I felt that loyalty to all our employees. That loyalty was built from a mutual trust that we tried to instill in the MTG culture—trust of course, is built over time, but may be shaken in an instant. Don had this conversation with me about loyalty. At some point, he said, loyalty has to switch from the individual employees to the organization itself.

"In a way, it hurt, but in a way it made sense—the best interests of the employees were really served by making sure the organization was in the best possible shape. Even when it meant an individual might suffer.

"I just couldn't stand the idea that it would be Don that would suffer," Tom said. "In the end, I did have loyalty to him, and he didn't suffer.

"When I ran across a couple of guys that reminded me so much of myself and Jose in our early years—fumbling around, on the verge of either big success or utter failure—I was so happy to hook them up with Don. He and I knew he had a purpose with them. It was great."

"And Rachel?" someone asked.

"Well, not quite so satisfying," Tom admitted. "She wasn't all that happy and it wasn't all that easy to help her find a job.

But she did have to go, she was more than irritating—she was holding her people back.

Success can throw you up against the ropes almost as hard as failure.

"There were about two years in there that I felt like we were lost—it reminded me of my first year at college. I was so anxious to get away from home, to strike out on my own.

Then I was away and it seemed like stuff I'd always had a handle on at home was now out of control."

He went to the whiteboard. "And that's *BreakPoint Six*," he said. "You're almost down for the count. Just when you think you've got it made, Mike Tyson comes into the ring and bites your ear off.

"It's not fatal but it shocks the hell out of you," he continued. "You stagger around for a while before you pull yourself together and hit back. Believe it not, success can throw you up against the ropes almost as hard as failure." Tom saw that most of the class looked puzzled.

"We pulled out of it together. We brought a great CFO on board—but not until after we hired a guy who didn't work out—and we found a hotshot HR person who cracked a velvet-covered whip.

"I'm serious. The whole atmosphere—the pace of the company—picked up when we got the rest of the management team up to the level of Melanie and Walter. Suddenly we were turbocharged. And, as I'm sure I've said before, a Maserati doesn't handle like a Mustang.

"Don't forget. Jose and I weren't like you hothouse flowers—we were old school. When Walter started talking about stack ranking and variable compensation plans for engineers, we only knew vaguely what he was talking about.

"We did miss that—I guess you'd call it that family feeling. Up until a few years before Walter came, Jose and I knew everyone at MTG—knew them, not just their names. I always interviewed every candidate before they were hired. I personally knew everything that was going on all over the company. And then one day, I didn't—couldn't.

"A few years earlier, maybe more than I really recall, Jose and I had agreed that our ultimate goal was to sell the business and be in a position where we never had to work again, if we didn't want to. But we didn't want to leave MTG in the lurch. This meant we had to make some financial decisions that were better for us in the long-term than in the short-term.

"Like putting $300,000 into new systems for HR and accounting. We didn't want to just cobble together the old system with duct tape and Ethernet glue. We wanted to sell a company we could be proud of, not a fixer-upper." Tom went to the whiteboard to summarize the next *BreakPoint*:

BreakPoint #6: Changing the Guard

- Upgrade the management team.

- Embrace expertise and specialization.

- Invest in systems that can grow to the next level.

- Realize that loyalty now rests with the company, not the individual.

— The Last Class —

BREAKPOINT #7
CEO Time

Leadership and learning are indispensable to one another.

Boys and girls! Guys and gals! Ladies and gentlemen! Let's get this show on the road so we can all get down to McGurk's for a couple of Schlaflys on the company tab.

"I trust you're all impatient to start your engines and roar into the future at the wheel of your own entrepreneurial vehicle …"

Tom stopped. His students were rolling their eyes. "A little heavy on enthusiasm and the racing analogy?" he asked.

"Not to mention the clichés," someone answered.

"Okay, let's get down to it," Tom continued. "We're on the final chapter. I'm going to go over the six *BreakPoints* we've covered, then swing into the last one.

"But before I do that," he said. Eyes rolled again.

"Before I do that," Tom repeated, "I want to remind you all of something that is a key aspect of every single *BreakPoint*. And that is:

Ask for help.
Seek mentors.

137

"Very, very few people can create a business, let alone grow one, without help. As Don would say—as he often said—'The school of hard knocks is no place to be alone in a corner.'"

"There are a lot of people just like me, who will be happy to show you their entrepreneurial scar tissue and share their experience if they believe you are sincere about learning from them.

"By taking this class, by recognizing that you want to do more than work for yourself—that you want to create a business—you're ahead of the game. In fact, you are already showing signs of ... wait for it ... you are showing signs of making a plan."

Tom waved away the groans and kept going. "And that swings us right into ..."

He went to the white board and wrote.

BreakPoint #1: Make a Plan

- Decide the mission of your business.

- Decide what you want out of life and what you are willing to do—and to give up—to get it.

- Develop the road map to get there.

"If you want to build a business, you have to know where you're headed and how you are going to get there. Notice my emphasis on the second half of that sentence: 'How you are going to get there.'

"Choosing your destination is only the first step in planning, which is a separate exercise. As Harvey McKay says, 'A goal without a plan is just a dream.'"

He scrawled again on the whiteboard.

BreakPoint #2: Building Your Pit Crew

- Recruit the best.

- Invest in the hiring process.

- Let people do their jobs within the structure you've created.

"People will be your major assets. The same rule applies to hiring as to buying art or antiques: Get the best you can find and afford. Take your time, do your homework, consult your experts. Always keep your eyes open for prospects.

"And please, people, remember—the hiring process isn't over until it's over. Don't leave your bright shiny new guys at the door. Bring them on board; make them feel connected.

"Do that and you've got a much better chance of keeping a good employee. Invest in their comfort and productivity; they'll invest in you.

"Second point," he continued. "Follow Patton's advice: Don't tell people how to do things. Tell them what to do and let them surprise you with the results.

"The surprises won't always be happy. But let people do their jobs. Let 'em learn from their mistakes. When you have to, let 'em do a job 85 percent as well as you would do it.

"At some point, someone is going to do the job 100 percent better than you can. And that's exactly what you want."

BreakPoint #3: Communicating on Purpose

- Learn your communication style.

- Learn how to improve one-on-one communications.

- Use communications to improve the effectiveness of your leadership team.

- Learn how to communicate to large groups, inside and outside of your organization.

Tom turned from the whiteboard, capping his marker.

"If I had to devote a semester to just one breakpoint, it would be this one," he said, "that's how crucial it is to create an atmosphere of open communication.

"At MTG, we had the benefit of working with Jo Murphy. There are a lot of behavioral assessment tools out there and I've done them all—DISC, Myers-Briggs, Predictive Index, Caliper and probably a dozen others. The key is finding someone like Jo to interpret the results, someone who can show you how to use them.

"I can't say enough about how these insights changed the way I see people. I understand them better. I understand myself better.

"Knowing that, using that understanding to communicate more effectively, has made all my relationships richer. It's helped me focus on people for their strengths, rather than their faults. That encourages candid debate and disagreement, an atmosphere where ideas flourish.

"Easier said than done, but the end results are absolutely worth it."

BreakPoint #4: Partnership Pain

- "Date" long enough to know the "marriage" will last.

- Talk money, skills and values.

- Sign a "pre-nup" to cover the end of the partnership.

"Partnerships are very much like marriages—without the benefit of sex to smooth the rough spots," Tom said.

"Don't get married in a fever—you'll regret it. Take your time getting into the relationship, consider alternatives and make plans for a graceful exit."

BreakPoint #5: Revving the Engine

- "Best salesperson" does not equal best "sales manager."

- Develop a recruiting/hiring process.

- Know the numbers you need to succeed.

- Use every available sales avenue.

"Do not take your most productive salesperson and turn her into your sales manager," Tom said, turning to the class.

"The skill set isn't the same—and it's incredibly hard to replace the production of your top representative. She or he can't cover both jobs.

"It's easy to track sales on the back of an envelope when you're small. When you're big, you need a system, you need goals, you need a way to measure results.

"Stay ahead of the game," he continued. "Get farm teams going, so you've got players warming up in the bullpen. Stay in touch with the up-and-comers—they're going to know about Facebook, Twitter and who knows what's next before you do. Do whatever it takes to feed the beast."

BreakPoint #6: Changing the Guard

- Upgrade the management team.

- Embrace expertise and specialization.

- Invest in systems that can grow to the next level.

- Realize that loyalty now rests with the company, not the individual.

"Success—the point when the business takes a giant leap forward—can be the toughest part," Tom said, sitting on the edge of a desk. "Just when you're thinking how great everything is, you realize you may have bitten off more than you can chew.

"It's like moving up to a D1 league with a D3 team. You scramble for a game or two, but if you're going to play at that level consistently, you've got to recruit better players. Unlike college, your best guys aren't going to move on after four years so you can replace them. You have to transition them out—otherwise, the team will fail.

"Worse, it might be you or your partner that needs to be upgraded," he said. "It's grueling.

"And that," Tom said, "brings us to…"

BreakPoint #7: CEO Time

"Have you ever thought about what a CEO does? I mean, what's the purpose, when you've got a great management team on board and the machine is clicking?

"Think about it—what does a CEO do?"

There was a silence in the room. Tom, one leg swinging off the edge of the desk, let the quiet linger for several seconds.

"Go ahead. Google the definition," he said. "It'll say something like 'The CEO is the executive responsible for the company's operations, for coordinating external business and internal operations so that the two align according to the vision or mission of the company.' Got that?"

He paused again. "What the hell does that mean?"

Tom got up, stuck his hands in his pockets and began to pace in the front of the room.

"I've given this a lot of thought," he said.

"When the management team gelled, I didn't have operational responsibilities anymore. I had to redefine my role in the business—and I had to do it without getting in the way.

"Where was my value? Or to put it in today's jargon, what value was I adding since I was no longer responsible for sales or implementation?"

He went to the whiteboard and wrote a single word:

Leadership

"That's what I came up with—my role was to lead MTG in a way that was different from building the company. Like a lot of guys, I'd been so tied up chasing sales or putting out fires for 12 years that I had never focused on leadership or tried to define it.

"It hit me that MTG wasn't about just me and Jose anymore. It was about 150-some people who'd built their lives and lifestyles around the stability of their jobs at MTG, who were depending on me to keep this company on track for them.

"When I started trying to define leadership, I came across a thought from John F. Kennedy that put me on the right track:

Leadership and learning are indispensable to one another.

"I'd been learning all along, mostly as a survival tactic. Now that MTG was clicking along on its own, I had time to think about those lessons, learn more and put 'em together in a way I hoped would help me lead the company into the future."

Tom paused for a sip of water.

"I thought this quest to define leadership might be a real grind but it turned out to be completely satisfying—in fact, it's something I'm still pursuing and I will pursue for the rest of my life.

"Here's what I've learned so far. Great leaders, in my mind, have several characteristics in common."

He put an image on the screen.

- Recognize, appreciate and reward talent.
- Communicate clearly.
- Establish priorities.
- Demand accountability.
- Empower others to achieve their goals.

Tom's favorite student raised her hand. "Aren't those almost the same things you do to grow the business?" she asked.

"Essentially, yes," he said. "And doing them winds up creating the sixth characteristic of a great leader—though it's not something they do. It's something they earn. Loyalty."

He put another image up on the screen, a circular puzzle with six interlocking pieces labeled trust, relationship, empathy, understanding, knowledge and loyalty.

"You can't demand loyalty. It's organic. It depends on trust, which, of course, can only develop in a relationship. That, naturally, depends on empathy and understanding, which grows out of knowledge between the people in a relationship.

"It's what I call the loyalty puzzle. The key to the puzzle is knowing what people want out of life—and then helping them get it. People work harder when they know that you care about their lives and want them to reach their goals, as well as the company goals. Great leaders earn loyalty because they focus as much on the goals of others as on their own.

"And I'm convinced that loyalty doesn't stop at the company doors. Loyalty to and from your customers and your suppliers, as well as the companies you need to support your growth— those loyalties are just as important to success. You want them to be there for you. You have to, from time to time, be there for them, too.

"To paraphrase Peter Drucker, 'The leaders who work most effectively never say 'I.' They don't think 'I,' they think 'we,' they think 'team.' They take responsibility, but the team gets the credit. That creates trust and loyalty.'

"So that's pretty much what I've learned, so far, about leadership," Tom finished.

"I thought you were going to talk about becoming a CEO," said one student.

"And why you sold MTG," said another.

"Well, yeah, I am," said Tom, "but first I want to tell you about a golf game …"

"Yet another golf game," said one woman in a stage whisper.

"That's right, another golf game," Tom continued, "seems like the course at High Pines had become the backdrop of my business life.

"Anyway, on this particular day I was networking with a new contact, another business owner who brought along two of his associates—a banker and investor.

"They were 'suits' in the worst way. We'd just played the third hole when they started talking shop—roll-ups, mezzanine financing, the cost of capital. I'm thinking, I had a roll-up and coffee for breakfast and mezzanine financing is when you're too broke to buy box seats. I could feel brain freeze setting in.

"Seriously, those concepts weren't foreign to me. I just wasn't interested … to me, the finance, accounting and legal aspects of business are just painful necessities.

"By the start of the back nine, this nagging feeling I'd had for several weeks was starting to crystallize. I was more interested in the concept of leadership at the CEO level than in the day-to-day processes.

"Everything was about leverage—leveraging momentum, our brand, solutions, profit centers, funding decisions. I could learn all that stuff or I could hire whatever professional talent I needed to get the job done. I didn't want to. What I like about business is the building process, not 'positioning' and worrying about market share. But that's what MTG needed—what those 150-some employees who'd signed on with MTG needed."

So what makes a leader?

"I didn't decide anything on the course that day—except to never again golf with finance guys.

"Over the next few weeks, thinking about it and talking with Jose, it dawned on me that we had exhausted our 'entrepreneurial quotient.' Creating and building MTG had been exciting—chaotic, at times, yes—but really thrilling for most of the 14 or 15 years we'd been in business together. Now it was just stressful."

Tom stopped pacing.

"There's another aspect to leadership—not to mention life—and that's knowing when your skills are no longer what the company needs.

"Really, everything we've been talking about all along is observing, studying and analyzing what's going on with yourself, your people and your company. Knowing yourself is crucial.

"What this meant for me is acknowledging I was no longer the right leader for MTG. It was time for me to focus on what I was good at, rather than trying to lead the organization without the right skills. It was time to either sell or bring in a CEO who would be a better fit."

He took a seat again on the edge of a desk.

"Like I've said before, Jose and I had decided a few years earlier that we'd ultimately cash out. We knew it wouldn't be hard, over the past few years we'd had numerous buyout offers.

"What we didn't want was to sell to just any bidder with a bundle of money. I was really committed to finding somebody with the leadership qualities I'd learned about, the buyer that MTG deserved.

"It took awhile, but once word we were selling got out, we heard from someone who'd expressed interest some years earlier. Bill Green wanted to take his firm—about twice the size of MTG—into the business intelligence market. Jose's product fit his strategy perfectly.

"And he fit my picture of a great CEO, someone who would value MTG beyond its cash value. He courted us, we vetted him, several months went by while we hammered out details and went through due diligence, but the upshot was, we sold MTG to Bill's company. I signed an 18-month contract to cover the transition. And now I'm on to other things."

He stopped talking and looked at the class. More than a few seconds of silence passed, causing a few people to squirm.

"So what makes a leader? Some say a leader is a person you'd follow to a place you wouldn't go alone. For me, it goes beyond that—and I hope not only that I live up to this standard but that it's something you future leaders can strive toward. "I think John Quincy Adams nailed it—'If your actions inspire others to dream more, learn more, do more and become more, you are a leader.'

"There's a quote that I read a number of years ago that I always say when I finish a presentation or a meeting at MTG, a reminder to myself and everyone else:

'Business education without execution is just entertainment.'

"I hope that the last eight weeks have been more than just entertainment, that you will take what you have learned and put it to good use.

"I look forward to hearing about all of your successes in the future and I wish you the best of luck on your own entrepreneurial journeys...."

Where the Rubber
Meets the Road

Where the Rubber Meets the Road

*It's fine to celebrate success but it is more important
to heed the lessons of failure.*
Bill Gates

Growing a business from scratch is one of the hardest things you can do in life. But if you can build a successful business that fulfills your creative, financial and lifestyle needs, there is no more satisfying way of life. We know—"We" are Larry Kesslin and Chris Winter, principals of 4-Profit, a leadership development firm with a primary focus on IT solution providers. Over the course of our partnership, we've met thousands of business owners. We've worked with hundreds of them as clients, helping them develop stronger leadership skills and more profitable businesses.

Through those many years, our perception and understanding of business ownership and entrepreneurship has evolved into a concept we think is very different from the norm. The distinctions may seem subtle but, to us, they can make the difference between a business that is successful or a life that is richly satisfying. Too many business owners organize their lives to meet the needs of their business. At 4-Profit, we believe your business should be a vehicle that sustains and enhances your life.

Owning a business is a life choice that provides the possibility of living an extraordinary life—and you get to define extraordinary. If you take full advantage of that possibility, you may end up with a life transformed beyond your dreams. The biggest reward, in our minds, is the freedom to live your values.

Your goal may be to devote yourself to adventure; to contribute to the educational needs of a remote, undeveloped village; to spend more time at your child's soccer games or scouting expeditions; to fund scientific research or pursue an artistic career. You may aspire to be Steve Jobs and pursue technical and aesthetic perfection. You may follow Bill Gates and determine to eradicate malaria while bringing the Internet to every child in the world. Or pursue personal tax equality like Warren Buffet did.

Whatever the scope or scale of a business owners' dreams, we have never met a one who wasn't searching, in one way or another, for a sustainable business to provide a bit more freedom.

That's the reason we started 4-Profit and wrote *BreakPoints*; to help you get past the sticking points and reach your goals.

As Tom said in *BreakPoints*, the first step toward success and the resulting freedom is to answer this question: "What do I want my life to look like?" For many, the answer isn't so clear.

Some business owners get stuck for years, and even decades at certain BreakPoints.

You don't have to come up with an answer immediately. And the answer quite likely will evolve over time. But you are more likely to end up at your desired destination if you have an idea of what it looks like. Write it down. Draw a picture of it. Make it a mantra or a touchstone that you can return to, especially when faced with a decision that seems problematic. Pull out your touchstone then, your mantra or your drawing, and ask yourself: "Which decision will take me closer to my destination?" If you don't know where you are going, and you don't have a guide, there is no clear reason to make one decision over another.

If you don't have a destination in mind, your first instinct may be to build a business just to make money. In the long run, that approach may leave you rich but still lusting for freedom and purpose. "I'll be happy when ...." is a pretty big red flag for this thinking. Financial reward should be the byproduct of a good business model, executed well. If you start with the problem you want to solve, and with the end in mind, your chances of success are vastly increased.

Some business owners get stuck for years, and even decades at certain *BreakPoints*. At 4-Profit, we have developed a coaching process that we call *The 4-Profit Way*. This process helps our coaches identify the root cause of the challenge facing our clients. Most of our clients just want to know what to do next, but it is not always that easy.

Over the years, we have identified the differences between business owners, entrepreneurs and chief executive officers (CEOs). Most individuals are not CEOs, not by a long shot. The average business owners and entrepreneurs typically don't have the wisdom, experience and discipline to be excellent CEOs. And that is where so many of them—especially entrepreneurs—get stuck in growing their businesses. The attributes of a CEO versus a business owner are found in their ability to create sustainable scale. Unfortunately, these skills are not automatic or guaranteed—they don't come with a title. Are CEOs born or made? The answer is that they are born with traits that must be shaped, nurtured, coached and mentored.

We distinguish between entrepreneurs, business owners and CEOs by asking a few key questions:

- Are the owners capable of leading this organization?

- Are the owners in the right roles for their skill set?

- Are the owners taking compensation based on their contribution to the business or because of their power to write checks to themselves?

- Are the owners taking responsibility for success by adjusting their personal pay when the business is in a decline or they make a mistake that affects the business?

- Are the owners capable of taking the business to the next level?

If you own a business and you understand the difference between equity, compensation and role, then you can develop a business that can attract the best talent.

Do you own the business to feed your ego or to meet the needs of your clients and your life? If you are the owner of the business and believe you need to be the CEO but don't have the skills to do the job, you are reducing your chances of success.

If you become clear about what you do and why (this is a big "if"), and then you can modify your behavior (an even bigger "if"), then ownership can lead to great results. If you don't understand the root cause and the depth of your challenges, you will get, and remain stuck. The *BreakPoints* become the norm.

We've known business owners who've been wildly successful and have seen others fail needlessly. Mostly, though, we've seen owners whose businesses are just stuck. They can't find their way to the next stage of growth and prosperity. They haven't found the right business model. They haven't been able to recruit at the next level of talent. Their internal systems don't operate smoothly. They have hit a BreakPoint on the path to success.

Over the years, we've realized that our clients—and other business owners—all seem to struggle with the same obstacles. That's why we decided to write *BreakPoints*. To convey to others how to recognize those key breaking points and some of the ways we've developed to overcome the most common obstacles. Our book is about how to build bridges, clear rubble and provide alternate routes to overcome the *BreakPoints*.

These are solutions that can be applied to any industry. Whether your ultimate goal is to sell your company for a whopping pay-off or to create a business that will comfortably sustain your family for decades to come, we hope our book prompts you to look at your business from a different perspective.

If you are a business owner feeling stuck, *BreakPoints* may provide insight about the source and illuminate a path to get you moving again. If you don't yet own a business, we think our book will provide guidance for avoiding the *BreakPoints* altogether. Even if your business is running smoothly, we hope you'll be prompted to evaluate your business—and your life—

to ensure both are as effective, productive and enjoyable as possible.

There is one business obstacle that we purposefully did not include in *BreakPoints* and that is the issue of cash flow. Everyone asks us why not? As we said in one of the earlier chapters, managing cash flow is a given, not a *BreakPoint*. If you don't manage cash flow from the start—and every single day after—you won't make it to the *BreakPoints*! You must have a solid and vigilant understanding of finance, beyond being able to balance your checkbook. Finance includes issues of investment, reward, profit margin, expense management, goal setting, equity management and succession planning. In *The 4-Profit Way* we keep these issues at the forefront for ourselves and for our clients.

We realize that no one book can provide all the solutions to creating and sustaining a great company. And we realize that *BreakPoints* represents, by necessity and style, more of an example to consider rather than an explicit roadmap to follow.

Execution is far more important than getting the road map exactly right. We can offer the same compensation plan to three different companies and often get three very different receptions for those plans. The difference is in the delivery, how leadership presents the plan and how the employees perceive it.

In some chapters, we've had to simplify the solutions reached by Tom and Jose. So, to give you more specifics to contemplate, we've gone through the book, *BreakPoint* by *BreakPoint*, and come up with steps to help you focus more sharply on identifying and reaching your destination.

BreakPoint 1:
Charting Your Course

A goal without a plan is just a wish.
Antoine de Saint-Exupery

A business is a vehicle to help you meet the needs of your life, not the other way around. That's easy to forget when you are in the throes of starting your own business—especially if you haven't figured out:

a) what you want your life to look like, and

b) why you are going into business.

A great financial return is the outcome of an effective business plan to please, and actually *delight*, your clients at a reasonable price. You want your client to not question the value of your service—you want them to cherish the relationship and what you do. The better your service, the better your returns. When well executed, a good business plan will result in financial gain. But if you establish a business only for financial gain, you'll find it very challenging to motivate others to join your cause. Pure financial goals aren't, in the long run, sustainable.

If money is your motivation, your employees will follow your lead and more regularly ask themselves "What's in it for me?" Your business will be better positioned if it has a mission beyond just making money. People want to believe they are part of a cause—even something as simple as making the best ice cream.

Or maybe your mission is helping people connect in better ways than they could before, by producing new information technology products.

There is always a great mission to strive toward—and sometimes more than one. You may dedicate some part of your company's effort toward a local cause, as well as your commercial mission. Listen to what your people are passionate about and develop a business based on purpose, not money.

A final suggestion: add one more ingredient—a plan for getting out of the business, an exit or succession plan. You're thinking this is a daunting task without a crystal ball, but your exit or end game will influence the decisions you make along the way. And there is always the possibility of the unexpected event that may force you out of business.

We want *BreakPoint #1* to prompt you to assess your goals in life; your reasons for going into business for yourself, and what you want the business to accomplish; and, ironically, how you see your eventual exit from the business.

1. Write a personal mission statement that describes the life you want to live and the values you want to communicate through the way you live and do business.

2. Write a mission statement for your business. Describe—briefly—what you want the business

to accomplish, its reason for existence. What picture would you like others to paint about you and your success when you retire?

3. Meet with your executive team, partner or other key people connected to your business to discuss your mission. Meet away from the office—your session is to work on your business, not in the business. It should result in much more than a statement posted on the wall of a cubicle or screen saver. Your mission statement should be repeated or reflected in every major action or communication you make internally. And, if you are accomplishing great things within and outside your company, let others know about it.

Write a simple one- or two-page business plan. Create your "100 day plan" outlining manageable increments with specific targets you can accomplish in that time period. Review your progress every month or, for larger organizations, at least every quarter.

A corporation is a living organism; it has to continue to shed its skin. Methods have to change. Focus has to change. Values have to change. The sum total of those changes is transformation.
Andrew Grove

BreakPoint 2: Building Your Pit Crew

You're only as good as the people you hire.
Ray Kroc

People are your most important asset, period!

Hiring is one of the most important roles of a leader. Yet so many skimp on time and effort spent evaluating and recruiting new employees. If you were going to spend $100,000 on a piece of equipment or software, wouldn't you invest weeks or even months making the decision? Put the same effort into hiring and training key employees.

Yes, you say, but we're a small company and can't afford to hire the best. Wrong. At 4-Profit, we have seen the difference between average and great talent, and you can't afford to hire average. Top employees often out-produce average employees by a magnitude of two to five—if not more. You can't afford not to hire the best you can afford at every stage of your business. Then "upgrade" them by providing learning and training opportunities. If they are not "upgradeable" or they don't have the skills that your growing and/or changing organizational needs, they need to be moved out.

You may be thinking of compensation in terms of money alone. Recent findings by the Gallup Organization indicate that "… money is losing its power as a central motivator, in part because the general population is realizing, in greater numbers, which—above a minimum level necessary for survival—money adds little to their subjective well-being."

Before you hire, ask yourself:

- Do I know what I want the person in this position to accomplish?
- How will this position evolve?
- Are there appropriate written job descriptions, so that my hire knows what is expected and can meet those expectations?

Top people want to strive toward a mutual goal and improve themselves. They also want a view of their future career path.

- **Be choosey in who you hire and be diligent in making new hires comfortable in your culture.**
- **Be clear on your expectations of employees and recognize and reward them for their accomplishments.**
- **Do not hire from a pool of one.**
- **Always be recruiting.**

One of the hardest of hard decisions you will make in business is to fire a good and loyal employee. In most cases, but for a variety of reasons, she or he has been there for a long time. For the sake of the business, they are no longer a fit.

- **Be prepared to take people out.**

Building a great team is work, so get to work and find the best people. Don't settle for anything less.

1. Assess your current talent and grade them A, B or C. Over the next 12 to 18 months, plan to improve or remove anyone who is not an A player.

2. Create a recruiting process. Build a simple file or wish list of people and behavioral types you would like to hire, their qualifications and potential positions.

3. Stress the importance of continual recruiting to key employees. The best source for employees is your existing employees.

4. Develop a screening tool and implement behavioral interviews to assess applicants. Find a GREAT resource to screen the testing results.

5. Develop an on-boarding process that begins with greeting new employees on their first day and getting them settled into their positions—with the help of a company mentor, if necessary.

6. Assess your system of rewards and incentives. Is it firmly anchored in job descriptions? Take advantage of employee strengths, rather than focusing on fixing weaknesses.

Start with good people, lay out the rules, communicate with your employees, motivate them and reward them. If you do all those things effectively, you can't miss.
Lee Iacocca

BreakPoint 3: Communicating on Purpose

Sometimes, I think my most important job as a CEO is to listen for bad news. If you don't act on it, your people will eventually stop bringing bad news to your attention and that is the beginning of the end.
Bill Gates

If communication isn't your highest priority, you might as well close your business and get yourself a job right now. That's how important it is to communicate—with your executive team, within your company and with the external community. And we're not talking quarterly newsletters.

Failure or inability to communicate is one of the two biggest obstacles to business success (the other is the inability to build a sales engine).

Every successful business leader we've ever spoken with cites the vital importance of understanding human behavior and communicating to employees based on that understanding. A fair number of them also articulate how important it is to start by understanding yourself—how you think, how you communicate and how you hear and respond to what others communicate.

We have come across some amazing resources. One standout is Jo Anne Myers (she's the inspiration for the Jo Murphy character). Jo Anne taught us how important it is to know our own style of communication and how it meshes—or conflicts—with the styles of others. Knowing that helps us avoid conflicts.

We have a concept called The 4 C's—four levels of communication—illustrated in the megaphone image below. The first C—C1— is learning about yourself and your communication style, what works and what gets in your way. Then learn to communicate with people with different styles and motivations. This is C2. A true leader learns to interact powerfully with those who see the world differently.

The third C: After mastering one-to-one communication, move to building good communication habits within the leadership team. Those habits will get you through rough times such as partnership break-ups or changing the guard. *The 5 Dysfunctions of a Team* by Patrick Lencioni is an excellent resource for understanding this concept.

The final C—C4—is communicating to large groups, directly and indirectly, those that work for you and those in your community. To reach everyone, use various modes to communicate because not everyone hears messages optimally in the same way.

Communication snafus deserve a book of their own. Until then, know that it's not enough to just say what your plans are, or what your mission is, or what you expect of employees. You have to live it. And embed your values, your strategies and tactics in the policies and practices of your company, so that employees live the mission, too—without having to give it much thought.

1. Know your communication or decision-making style. Find someone like Jo Anne Myers to help you.

2. Define your mission—clearly, with sharp focus—and communicate it often. Make it clear to each employee what his or her role is in achieving the mission—how important they are!

3. Embed your values in your policies and practices. If you say "cross-departmental cooperation is vital to success," link the goals and compensation packages of the departments, so they are bound to cooperate. Identify and break down imposed or cultural silos.

4. Encourage discussion, debate and disagreement within the executive team. Once a decision is made, the team should act as a single unit.

Communications is not about what you say
but what others hear.
Andrew Grove

BreakPoint 4: Partnership Pain

It is rare to find a business partner who is selfless.
If you are lucky, it happens once in a lifetime.
Michael Eisner

Business partnerships are challenging, even under the best of circumstances. There are any number of forms of partnership agreements. Familiarize yourself with the options—with the help of an attorney, a financial advisor and a coach—or all three.

Have a written partnership agreement. Period.
Double exclamation point!!

Before you finalize a partnership, even with your best friend, discuss how your decision-making styles mesh, what each of you wants from the business, and whether you are in agreement on how to make financial decisions.

Even good partnerships, like good marriages, have rough spots. Appreciate your partner's gifts and avoid focusing on weaknesses. If you have clarity about one another's roles, and communicate effectively, you should be able to get through troublesome times.

If, however, the partnership must end, make the arrangements quickly and cleanly. (An exiting mechanism MUST be spelled out in the original partnership agreement!) Each party should have separate legal representation.

1. "Date" before getting married. Have thorough discussions with potential partners about their goals

and expectations as well as your own. Get to know them, their values, and how they see money and other aspects of life before the courtship proceeds.

2. Put your partnership terms in writing. Include language to guide dissolution of the partnership—under both positive and negative circumstances.

3. Know one another's communication style and communicate regularly. Partnerships take work!

Failures don't plan to fail; they fail to plan.
Harvey MacKay

BreakPoint 5: Revving the Engine

A salesman, like the storage battery in your car, is constantly discharging energy. Unless he is recharged at frequent intervals, he soon runs dry. This is one of the greatest responsibilities of sales leadership.
R.H. Grant

Inability to manage sales growth and develop a scalable, reproducible sales engine is the place where most businesses get stuck. In *BreakPoints*, Tom and Jose solved the problem very simply by hiring a hot-shot sales manager with a good track record. While we implied that she had a process for training sales representatives and improving their productivity, we didn't go into her methods. Again, sales management is a topic that can—and does—fill many books.

The key point is that great sales people are not necessarily great sales managers. The skill sets for the two jobs are different. Many times the best sales managers are mediocre sales people who love to learn and love seeing others grow. A great sales manager—like most great leaders—thrives on the success of others. Not everyone can hire the ideal sales leader, able to produce predictable, scalable revenue. But you should at least know you are looking for someone who can appreciate and motivate the sometimes delicate, volatile or egocentric psyche of the sales force.

If you can't afford a sales manager at the moment, then you need to play that role. In addition, if you want to increase the revenue of your current team, it might be more productive to provide an assistant for your top producers than to ramp up new sales reps from scratch. It is easier to help a good producer increase his or her sales by 30 percent than it is to ramp up a new person from scratch. Hiring a support team for top performers will allow them to concentrate their efforts and energy on creating new sales rather than handling run rate business and necessary paperwork.

1. Don't make your best salesperson your sales manager!

2. Create a system of metrics to measure the production of each team member on an equal basis; in other words, compare final results to final results among the team members.

3. Standardize processes and systems to the extent possible. But work with each sales rep to take advantage of his or her strengths, rather than trying to convert everyone to an identical sales method.

4. Tie the goals and compensation packages of your marketing department, if you have one, to the results of your sales team. Studies show that sales leads and completed sales increase when sales and marketing are linked.

> *"If you don't know where you are going,*
> *any road will get you there."*
> Lewis Carroll

BreakPoint 6: Changing the Guard

The way a team plays as a whole determines its success.
You may have the greatest bunch of individual stars in the
world, but if they don't play together, the club won't
be worth a dime.
Babe Ruth

Building a business is not about winning as an individual. Building a business is about building a great team and winning as a team. As the business grows and changes, so does the team. It is inevitable that, during that process, some of the original team members either do not keep up with the growth or go in a different direction.

One of your biggest assets as an entrepreneur or business owner is the loyalty of your employees, mirrored by the loyalty you feel toward them. At some point, your loyalty must shift to the business itself, rather than any one individual. As difficult as it may be, your loyalty to the business will probably lead to recognition that a once-valuable team member is no longer valuable—and may even be a problem. If, like Don at MTG, the person is in agreement, count yourself lucky.

You are more likely to find yourself assessing an individual's contribution and find it coming up short.

You are in the unenviable position of transitioning that person either to another position or out of the company.

You do it with grace and as humanely as possible, but you must do it—for the good of the team.

That pain should be balanced by the great satisfaction of building a team of bright people, giving them the opportunity to put their strengths to optimal use, and teaching them to make decisions that help them achieve defined goals. Empowering others is something every leader should experience. Sometimes that means changing the players for the good of the team. You may be surprised when they thank you later on; your existing team will thank you even more.

1. Don't let misplaced loyalty inhibit your growth.

2. Recognize when a generalist needs to be replaced with a specialist, or when an individual needs to be replaced with a department!

3. Begin implementing standardized systems as early as you can; assess and adjust them periodically to manage your business and move it to the next level.

4. Reassess company strategy and the systems that support it at least once a year.

A goal is a dream with a deadline.
Napoleon Hill

BreakPoint 7: CEO Time

The best executive is the one who has sense enough to pick good men to do what he wants done, and self-reliant enough to keep from meddling with them while they do it!
Theodore Roosevelt

The CEO is the spider at the center of the corporate web. A very brief list of the CEO's responsibilities include:

- Develop the company's mission and set strategy to achieve it.

- Align all divisions of the company, and employees, behind the vision and strategy.

- Build company culture, by living—not just communicating—company values.

- Lead the executive team in defining the tasks needed to carry out the strategy, and assign responsibility for those tasks.

- Make final decisions on hiring and firing leadership team members.

- Allocate capital and make key financial decisions that meet the owners profitability and life goals in privately held companies.

Theodore Roosevelt's quote is apropos for all CEOs—get the best on your team and then get out of their way. If you have been learning as you build your business, you may have acquired the equivalent of an MBA and be fully qualified to manage and lead your company as CEO. If, however, you have been scrambling all along to keep the balls in the air, or you feel you have done an adequate job, but know that someone else can do it better, it may be time to let someone else do the job. If so, put your ego aside and get the right person in place. (If you feel you can be the best CEO, but need some help—by all means, get it.)

"Huh?" you may be thinking, "I got this far, why would I step aside now?"

You may step aside for the same reason you move another key person out of his or her job—because someone else can do it better and move the company to a new level. If you are that person who needs to move, you owe it to the company to get the better person in place.

As always, we feel the key to being in business for yourself is to put your best skills to use, to produce or create something that stirs the soul and makes you proud and then to foster the life you want to live. We've learned a lot from our own entrepreneurial journey. We hope the lessons in *BreakPoints* enhance yours and help you follow your passion.

The question of who ought to be boss is like
'Who ought to be the tenor in the quartet?'
Obviously, the man who can sing tenor.
Henry Ford

Acknowledgments

We would like to thank our wives, Ilise and Katie, and our children Drew, Noah, Sean and Maggie for their patience and support of the entrepreneurial way of life. Our families have been very patient through long hours in various business development endeavors over the past 15 years. As you all know, when you have your own business, you can never really turn it off. This balance between work and family is always a work in progress. While business can be exciting, we cannot buy back time and, although we are not always successful, we try to be present with precious time spent with family. We greatly appreciate the efforts and sacrifices made by these very special people and can't thank them enough for their support and encouragement.

In addition to her role as wife and mother, Ilise Kesslin was instrumental in the initial formation of this book. Without our early brainstorming sessions, along with her dedication and editing skills, we never would have completed our first draft.

We would also like to thank our co-writer, Susan Caba, for all of her efforts and ideas through this process. Susan's ability to create and hone the characters in this book, along with her ability to translate our thoughts into digestible words was amazing! In addition to Susan, we need to thank Judith Briles, our book shepherd. Without Judith and the resources she has brought to the project, including Nick Zelinger, you would not be holding this beautiful book in your hands right now!

THANK YOU!

4-Profit Team

We would also like to thank our 4-Profit team, including Jo Anne Myers (the inspiration behind Jo Murphy), Michael Schmidtmann (the inspiration behind the Melanie Stephens character), Frank Albi, Ginger Clay, Andy Gorelik, Scott Goemmel, Celia Harper-Guerra, Ronni Hendel-Giller and all of our clients who have been our best teachers. We are very excited about the future of our business and the support of these extremely talented individuals.

Contributions

Finally, we would like to thank the many entrepreneurs and industry leaders that have supported our programs over the past dozen years. We have had the pleasure to work with more than 1,000 solution providers over that time and delivered programs on behalf of numerous distributors and manufacturers. We look forward to working with many more talented individuals and leadership teams in the future.

About the Authors

Larry Kesslin is the CEO of 4-Profit LLC, a premier business coaching organization following a highly focused teaming approach called "The 4-Profit Way." We guide and inspire business leaders to reach their chosen business destination. Before starting 4-Profit, he worked at GE and Westinghouse.

Larry earned his BSEE degree from Rutgers University. At an early age, he knew that entrepreneurship was his passion. That has evolved to helping others meet their life goals on their entrepreneurial journey. Larry also spends significant time helping young social entrepreneurs around the globe avoid the same challenges our IT clients face every day.

In addition to his coaching and consulting work, Larry is a sought after public speaker.

Chris Winter, MBA, is a co-founder and principal of 4-Profit LLC. With an early career in IT including Xerox Corp., Chris lends his 15 years of experience and three privately-held businesses toward helping our clients and our 4-Profit team of coaches reach their full potential.

With a pure focus on helping businesses see "what's possible" whether in a lifestyle pursuit or optimizing a particular business model Chris has worked with hundreds of owners and leadership team members toward "better, better, better". It is with achievement and advancement that people can truly feel good about themselves and then enable success in others.

There is no greater thrill for Chris than a great "assist." To watch an athlete whether in sports, education or business, grow from the experience and training they receive and apply that knowledge to building something that will better themselves and those around them. He embraces life-long learning and seeks to share that knowledge as a coach whether it be for a business leader, golfer, basketball or soccer player.

Chris is very active in family and community and enjoys sports and the many parallels between the various teams we each play for in our lives.

About 4-Profit

4-Profit is an advisory services company working exclusively with IT solution providers, manufacturers and distributors with resources across the US. This is their second book, following up *Mastering a Culture of Accountability,* published in 2008.

www.4-Profit.com